Julie Le Clerc

MADE BY HAND

natural food to
nourish and delight

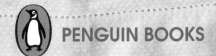
PENGUIN BOOKS

Ginger, pear & carrot chutney

"Food that nourishes us not only provides our body with the fuel and nutrients it needs, but can also provide emotional sustenance."

Dietary Requirements Key

DF DAIRY-FREE
EF EGG-FREE
GF GLUTEN-FREE
WF WHEAT-FREE
V VEGAN

Contents

Introduction

"I believe it is equally important that we eat for pleasure and for our health."

It is for this reason that I have put together this book of achievable, wholesome recipes using natural foods to nourish and delight. Food made by hand from natural ingredients definitely tastes superior. As a bonus, this sort of cooking is much better for us, as well.

A good recipe for health, happiness and longevity is really very simple. By getting back to eating unprocessed foods, using lighter cooking methods and following the seasons, we can all work towards improved eating habits and increased vitality.

While we all know what's good for us, sometimes it's nice to be gently reminded to do the obvious, such as: drink plenty of pure water every day; don't skip breakfast; take some time out for relaxation and pleasure; breathe; be more active; smile; enjoy cooking wholesome meals; and don't forget to garnish every dish with love.

This book is bursting with recipes to make using fresh, natural and easy-to-find ingredients. The notions behind these recipes will help you find healthier ways to enjoy some of your favourite foods, for example, by using healthy olive oil and less saturated fat in your cooking. With these recipes, I want to encourage everyone to reject highly processed, take-away and unhealthy snack foods and embrace deliciously natural foods made by hand.

But let's get one thing straight – this book is all about flavour, not sacrifice. Just because the food I am suggesting is natural, wholesome, light or gluten-free, does not mean it's boring or tasteless. Flavour has always been a firm focus for me when creating and developing recipes, and the recipes in this book are no exception. This book is about having your cake and eating it too — it's about combining vibrant flavours with wholesome ingredients to make food that will enhance, and perhaps prolong, your life.

By making even a few small changes every day, we can all work towards improved personal health and the health of our planet. It is such a simple way to bring about immense rewards. I'm not saying everyone must stop eating certain foods, and this is definitely not a diet book. However, you may find that by making a few small lifestyle changes and by using these recipes, you will experience weightloss naturally — as well as increased energy, reduced risk of developing major health problems and generally improved wellbeing. The impact of a few natural tweaks to our daily food intake can be amazing, even for people who already consider themselves to be healthy.

One of the most effortless actions we can all make is to increase our intake of fresh fruits and vegetables, fresh fish and whole grains. Eating a variety of fresh foods daily from different food groups is not just recommended, it's central to good health. Consuming a rainbow of different coloured fruits and vegetables every day really will help us live a brighter life.

Alongside caring about the food we eat, we also need to be conscious of the effect chemical cleaning agents are having on our health and the health of our environment. That's why I'm keen to share some of the alternative methods I've discovered for using cheap, everyday ingredients to keep your kitchen clean and well scrubbed without harsh chemicals. These ideas will help you get back to basics without using any extra elbow grease.

Activity is another vital part of the recipe for a good life. You may enjoy a daily brisk walk, some vigorous digging in the garden, or perhaps a sport, or dancing (that's what I enjoy most). Whatever kind of high-energy movement you add to your day will bring with it a strong sense of both physical and emotional wellbeing.

Finding a good balance between work and relaxation is important, too. I find cooking relaxing, even though it is my job, but I also know the benefits of a change of scenery when I'm feeling overloaded. Just taking time to relax and enjoy the company and conversation of friends and family can be very restorative.

Embracing organic and unprocessed wholefoods is the obvious way to ensure the food you eat is as natural as possible. While I don't expect everyone to become self-sufficient, I do believe we must pay more attention to where our food comes from and how it is grown. Planting a kitchen garden, or at the very least a few pots of herbs, is another good, honest place to start. You'll be richly rewarded for your efforts with not only fresh seasonal food, but a magical sense of pleasure and pride in your achievements. My own small plot has certainly brought me lots of joy over the years.

As I write this, sitting in my courtyard garden, I've just noticed the first tiny fruit buds on the small fig tree I have growing in a pot. A gift from a green-thumbed friend, I've been nurturing this tree for a couple of years now and so feel incredibly thrilled to see it bearing fruit for the first time. My mind is already full of ideas for how I might cook the anticipated dark velvety figs that I have encouraged to fruition.

> "This book is all about flavour, not sacrifice. Just because the food I am suggesting is natural, wholesome, light or gluten-free, does not mean it's boring or tasteless … This book is about having your cake and eating it too …"

Thinking about what we're eating leads me on to how we're eating. Many European cultures have known the value of slow food and slow eating for centuries. To join these enlightened people, all we need to do is slow down, pause and enjoy the aroma and texture of each morsel. Eating slowly and savouring every mouthful not only heightens our appreciation of our food, but also seems to alter time, slowing down life and calming us down, as well.

How and what we eat can also have an astounding effect on how we feel. Food that actually nourishes us not only provides our bodies with the fuel and nutrients they need, but because it tastes good, delicious food can also provide emotional sustenance. There are many dishes I can think of that make me nostalgic for my past. The current baking renaissance shows we all like to return to cherished childhood rituals and satisfying food experiences for the feelings of comfort they give us.

When I first began this book project, my focus was simply on cooking natural, fresh food, using organic ingredients when possible, and working with the seasons. My recipes have always been relatively healthy and light — except the sweet stuff, of course, which is not meant to be an everyday treat, so that's okay in the scheme of things. However, as I began to develop recipes based around this natural theme, I found my cooking continued to evolve and naturally became even lighter — but never at the expense of taste.

Feel free to use these recipes as springboards for your own ideas. Add whatever takes your fancy or whatever you have at hand. Leave out ingredients or make substitutions, if you wish. For instance, swap produce with the seasons or include vegetables you know your fussy-eaters will enjoy. Weave a little innovation into your own natural repertoire and I believe you'll be rewarded with more sensational meals.

A good place to start being more innovative in the kitchen is to ensure you have a well-stocked pantry. If you have a decent store of natural ingredients, like whole grains and pulses, natural baking ingredients, and a good array of flavourings, like spices, sauces, vinegars and oils, then good, healthy, everyday meals are so much easier to put together. To give you an idea of the crucial ingredients you might need to get started, I've included my list of priority pantry items on page 13.

I am not a nutritionist, but as a food writer and passionate chef, one important aspect of my work is continuing to extend my knowledge about food. I find the more I learn about natural foods, the more I want to cook with them and eat them. We all know what's good for us, but when we know why a food has health benefits then it makes good sense to eat more of it. That's why I made the decision to include small nuggets of information about the nutritional benefits of foods alongside the recipes. I hope this inspires you to add more vibrant, fresh produce and wholefood goodness to your everyday cooking.

You don't have to be a nutritional expert either to see that keeping it simple is the way to go. All we need to do is focus on eating foods as close to their natural state as possible — that is, fresh and unprocessed, and cooking these foods simply and well. I will show you how to add great natural flavour to recipes to make these already appetising foods taste even better.

These days we're exposed to a lot of information about foods, so much so that it's easy to feel overwhelmed. Sometimes trying to make sense of food messages can be exhausting, and trying to embrace a simpler life can seem to make life more complicated. That's why I've distilled a lot of information, so that it's easy to digest. It's just there to inspire you to cook with a wide range of wholefoods and natural delights. My hope is that these recipes will make cooking and eating good food, well, natural. And tasty!

Talking of new food trends, superfoods are super popular these days. 'Superfoods' is the media name given to a group of particularly nutrient-rich foods containing powerful antioxidants that can help delay ageing and disease and even enhance good moods. Whether or not we give them a label, some foods do seem to have more than their share of good attributes, and so eating more of these has got to be good for us. The list of so-called superfoods can differ and that's why I've based my superfood recipes around the most common top contenders.

I have to say, there's one food trend I've never followed and that is fast food. I find I never need to buy fast food, nor do I ever want to. Why would I when I can cook good, honest food for myself and my nearest and dearest, and gain huge pleasure at the same time? Though I can't deny some convenience foods are good and helpful, like canned organic tomatoes for use over the winter months when fresh tomatoes aren't great. Canned beans and chickpeas are also invaluable, because these can take a long time to prepare from scratch, as they need soaking overnight and long cooking.

Homemade is also the best, easiest and most cost-efficient way to make delicious sweet treats and puddings. I would even go as far as to say that baking can be a very therapeutic process — all that lovely creativity, nurturing warmth, comforting aromas and tastes. Plus, when you make it yourself, you know exactly what's gone into the food. While I have tried hard to ensure the sweet recipes in this book are healthier (though equally tasty) than other versions by reducing the sugar and fat contents overall, even the purest sweet treats should still be regarded as occasional foods.

At its heart, this book is about returning to a more wholesome, enjoyable way of cooking and eating at home. I've filled it with accessible recipes for you to make and share with your loved ones, so you can create fantastic food everyday using natural ingredients. Above all, I want to encourage you to get savvy and cook good, honest, tasty food from scratch, as this is a worthy and pleasurable skill that you can use to feed the people you care about.

Home cooking is so worthwhile, as it teaches us the importance of many things. A good home cook knows the value of wholefoods, fresh ingredients, and of cooking with the seasons. They know how to cook from scratch, and also how to make a fabulous thrifty meal from leftovers that can sometimes be even better than the first time around. They know how to provide nourishing food to keep bodies and minds happy, healthy and well fed. They know that healthy food does not need to be short on flavour, style or a sense of fun. They know the infinite value of food made by hand. And they know how to make the people they feed feel loved.

JULIE LE CLERC

"At its heart, this book is about returning to a more wholesome, enjoyable way of cooking and eating at home."

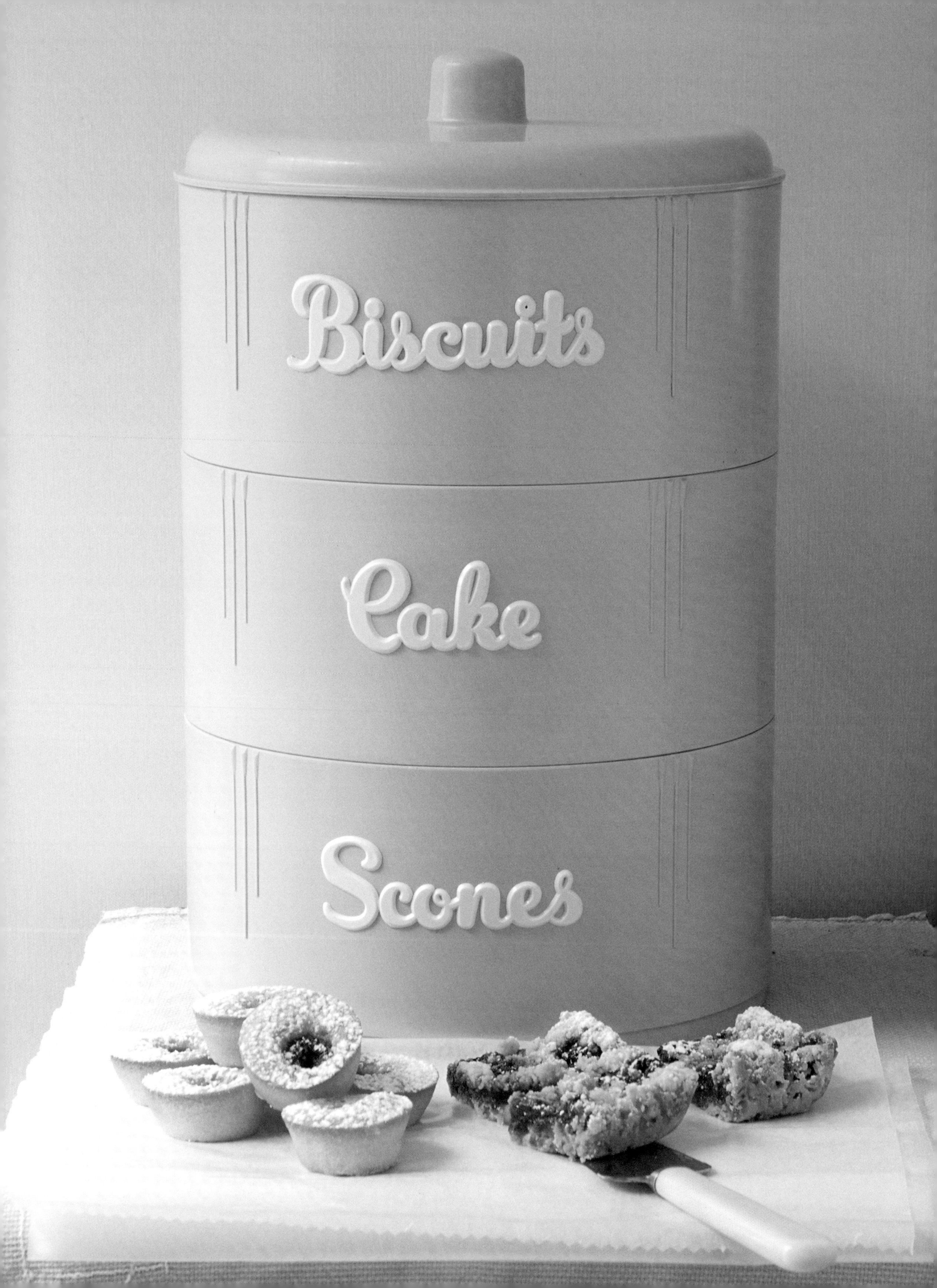
Biscuits
Cake
Scones

Quick Conversion Chart

Measures

1 level tsp (universal)	= 5 ml
1 level tbsp (NZ, UK, US)	= 15 ml
1 level tbsp (Australia only)	= 20 ml
1 cup liquid	= 250 ml
4 cups liquid	= 1 litre
1 pint	= 600 ml

Weights

30 g	= 1 oz
125 g	= 4 oz
225 g	= 8 oz
450 g	= 1 pound

Useful Equivalents

1 egg white	= 30 g
1 level cup flour	= 135 g
1 level cup sugar	= 200 g

Oven Temperature Guide *

	°C	°F	Gas Mark
Slow	110–130	225–250	½–1
Moderately slow	140–160	275–325	2–3
Moderate	180–190	350–375	4–5
Moderately hot	190–200	375–400	5–6
Hot	210–240	425–450	7–8
Very hot	250–260	475–500	9–10

* As oven models and thermostats vary, these conversions and the suggested recipe cooking times are a guide only. Fan-assisted (convection) oven temperatures need to be set lower than conventional oven temperatures. Increase the fan-assisted temperature given by 15 to 20 °C if using a conventional oven, or refer to the manufacturer's instructions.

The Natural Pantry

For any passionate cook, it's a really good idea to build a well-stocked pantry so that you always have supplies on hand to cook just about anything you desire, any day or night of the week.

This list is by no means definitive but it will give you a worthy starting point and includes the condiments and ingredients you will need most frequently. With these staple ingredients, and fresh seasonal produce, you will be able to cook any recipe in this book, entertain with ease, and prepare a variety of weekly meals in your own kitchen. I recommend choosing organic ingredients, whenever possible, so even though I do not always specify organic products here or in my recipes, please interpret organics as the preferred option.

Pantry Basics

Amaranth

Apple cider vinegar

Balsamic vinegar

Barley

Buckwheat

Bulghur wheat

Canned beans: red kidney, soy, black, cannellini and butter

Canned organic chickpeas

Canned organic tomatoes

Canned tuna, in spring water

Dried lentils: green, brown and red

Dried mushrooms: wood-ear, shitake and porcini

Dried split peas

Dried yeast

Extra virgin olive oil and other olive oil varieties (keep in dark bottles in a dark cupboard)

Light and dark soy sauce and wheat-free tamari

Millet

Mirin

Nori and other seaweeds

Old-fashioned rolled oats and whole oats

Polenta

Quinoa: white and red

Rice: basmati, brown rice and Italian risotto rice

Rice milk

Rice noodles and rice paper sheets

Salted capers

Sea salt and natural herb salt

Seeds: pumpkin, sunflower, flax and poppy

Soba noodles

Soy milk

Tamarind

Thai sweet chilli sauce

Whole-wheat pasta and other pastas

Baking Pantry

Baking soda

Cocoa powder

Cream of tartar

Dried fruits: raisins, sultanas, dates, figs, prunes, apricots and Craisins

Flours: baking, wholemeal, spelt, brown and white rice, tapioca, corn, buckwheat and gluten-free flour mix

Gluten-free baking powder

Maple syrup

Natural pure vanilla extract

Organic brown sugar

Organic honey

Palm sugar

Quality dark eating chocolate

Raw sugar

Rosewater

Vanilla beans

Wheat-free icing sugar

White and caster sugar

- - - - - - - - - - - - - - -

Spice Cupboard

Buy and grind in small amounts, as spices lose their potency with storage.

Allspice

Black peppercorns

Cardamom

Chilli flakes and powder

Cinnamon

Coriander seeds

Cumin seeds

Curry powder

Garam masala

Ginger

Paprika and smoked paprika

Turmeric

Wasabi powder or paste

Whole nutmeg

Yellow and black mustard seeds

- - - - - - - - - - - - - - -

In the Fridge

It is wise to store nuts and seeds and their oils in the fridge to keep them cool, as, when exposed to heat, these ingredients can easily turn rancid.

Ground almonds (almond meal)

Ground nut oils (such as walnut or hazelnut oil)

Miso

Mustards

Nut butters (such as peanut butter and almond butter)

Nuts: whole almonds, walnuts, pecans, hazelnuts, pine nuts (buy in small amounts and restock regularly)

Olives

Organic dried fruits (if your home is prone to weevils)

Organic or free-range eggs

Parmesan or Grana Padano

Sesame oil

Tahini

Thai fish sauce (if not used frequently, otherwise, store in a cool, dark cupboard)

Wholemeal flours

A note about parsley: I prefer to use flat-leaf parsley but curly works just as well and the taste is very similar

- - - - - - - - - - - - - - -

Natural Cleaning Products

Baking soda

Distilled white vinegar

Lemons

Food Terms

Al dente — just tender to the bite.

Almond meal (ground almonds)

Amaranth — the seed of a plant and ancient South American staple. Naturally gluten-free, highly nutritious and protein rich.

- - - - - - - - - - - - - - - -

Baking paper (parchment)

Baking soda (bicarbonate of soda / sodium bicarbonate)

Barley — a cereal grain with the outer husk removed (hulled). Pearl barley has been milled and is a polished form of the grain.

Beetroot (beets)

Broad beans (fava beans)

Buckwheat — highly nutritious seeds from a plant native to Russia and Northern Europe. The cooked seeds can be added to soups and stews or eaten in place of pasta or rice or as a salad.

Buckwheat flour — flour ground from wholegrain buckwheat.

Bulghur (burghul, bulgur) — wheat that has been boiled and dried and then ground into a fine, medium or coarse texture. Popular in Middle Eastern cookery.

Button mushroom (white mushroom)

- - - - - - - - - - - - - - - - - - - -

Cannellini beans (Italian white beans)

Capsicum (sweet bell pepper)

Caster sugar (superfine sugar)

Chickpea flour (besan) — flour made from ground chickpeas.

Coriander (cilantro)

Cornflour (corn starch)

Courgette (zucchini)

Couscous — a very tiny type of pasta made from semolina and flour (and therefore contains gluten), couscous is a staple dish of Morocco and Tunisia.

Craisins (dried cranberries)

- - - - - - - - - - - - - - - - - - - -

Dark cane sugar (dark muscovado sugar)

- - - - - - - - - - - - - - - - - - - -

Eggplant (aubergine)

En papillote — cooking food in a paper parcel.

- - - - - - - - - - - - - - - - - - - -

Field mushrooms (Portobello mushrooms / flat mushrooms)

Fish sauce — sauce made from fermented, salty fish, common in South-East Asian cooking.

Flat-leaf parsley (Italian parsley)

Flax seeds (linseeds) — highly nutritious seeds from a flax plant.

- - - - - - - - - - - - - - - - - - - -

Garam masala — an Indian spice blend usually containing ground coriander, cumin, cinnamon, cardamom, nutmeg and cloves.

Ghee (clarified butter) — popular in North Indian cooking, ghee can be heated to high temperatures without burning as butter would.

Glass noodles (cellophane noodles / bean thread noodles) — very fine dried noodles made from green mung bean starch. When cooked they are transparent and glass-like.

- - - - - - - - - - - - - - - - - - - -

Icing sugar (confectioners' sugar)

- - - - - - - - - - - - - - - - - - - -

Kecap manis — Indonesian sweet, thick soy sauce.

Kumara (sweet potato)

LSA — highly nutritious combination of ground flax seeds, sunflower seeds and almonds.

Millet — a cereal grass staple of Africa and Asia. Can be cooked and used in place of rice or pasta.

Mirin — Japanese sweet rice wine used to add sweetness to dressings, marinades and sauces.

Miso paste — made from fermented soya beans, miso paste forms the base of miso soup and can also be used as a condiment or in dressings and sauces.

Nori — paper thin sheets of edible seaweed used in Japanese dishes, such as sushi rolls.

Polenta (corn meal) — Italian corn meal that is traditionally cooked into a thick savoury porridge.

Porcini mushrooms — type of mushrooms, known as ceps in France. Sold dried and available from specialty food stores and good delicatessens.

Pulses (dried legumes) — dried, large edible seeds, such as lentils, various beans and peas.

Quinoa — an ancient type of grass seed native to South America. Quinoa is highly nutritious, protein rich, and naturally gluten-free and can be used in place of rice or pasta in many dishes.

Radicchio (Italian chicory) — Dark purple, bitter tasting endive.

Raw sugar (Demerara/light muscovado sugar)

Red onion (purple onion)

Rice flour — gluten-free flour made from ground white or brown rice.

Rice vermicelli noodles — very fine dried noodles made from rice flour (gluten-free) and water.

Rocket (arugula)

Rosewater — essence of roses made from distilled rose petals, rosewater adds flavour and perfume to baking and other dishes.

Shitake mushrooms — meaty-textured type of Asian mushroom, can be bought fresh or dried from Asian food stores.

Silver beet (Swiss chard)

Smoked salmon (lox)

Soba noodles — type of noodle made using mostly gluten-free buckwheat flour, though it is wise to check the ingredients list as they may also contain other gluten flours.

Soya beans (edamame)

Spelt flour — flour ground from spelt, an ancient form of wheat that is believed to be more easily digestible than modern wheat.

Spring onion (scallion / green onion)

Tahini — a thick paste made from hulled and ground sesame seeds, commonly used in Middle Eastern cookery.

Tamari — mellow flavoured, naturally fermented soy sauce, generally containing little wheat,

though some brands are wheat- and gluten-free.

Tamarind — a bean-like Asian fruit that is crushed to give a pulp that when mixed with water and strained makes tamarind water. Concentrated tamarind pulp can be bought from Asian food stores.

Tapioca flour (cassava flour) — gluten-free, fine flour ground from the cassava root and used as a thickener or in baking.

Thread coconut (shredded coconut)

Tofu (soya bean curd) — made from soya beans, compressed blocks of tofu can be either soft (silken) or firm. A good form of vegetable-based protein, tofu is bland-tasting but will take on other flavours it is mixed with.

Tomato sauce (tomato ketchup)

Wasabi powder — ground from the dried root of a Japanese aquatic plant, wasabi has a hot, pungent flavour often likened to horseradish.

Wood-ear mushrooms — a frilly, dark-coloured type of Asian mushroom. Highly nutritious, wood-ear mushrooms can be bought dried from Asian food stores.

Break of Day
good morning food

* Rise and shine. Greet each morning with gusto and break the fast with a big healthy bowlful of homemade cereal. Relish each mouthful of crunchy high-fibre grains mixed with luscious yoghurt and fresh, baked or poached fruits. Natural cereals kickstart your day and release their energy slowly, keeping you sustained longer.

Or, breakfast on a simple, tasty egg dish that is protein-packed and guaranteed to keep you going. Do yourself a favour and make the time to savour breakfast, as enjoying good morning food really is the best way to power up your day.

Swiss-Style Bircher Muesli

I first learned how to make this fresh muesli when I lived in Switzerland, the birthplace of Bircher muesli, many years ago. Invented by and named after Swiss nutritionist, Dr Bircher-Brenner, this muesli is wonderfully healthy and yet tastes decadently creamy and delicious.

SERVES 4   EF | WF

1½ cups old-fashioned rolled oats
1½ cups apple juice, or any preferred juice
juice of 1 lemon
1 apple, grated with the skin on
1 banana, mashed
2 tbsp liquid honey

½ cup plain unsweetened yoghurt
¼ cup flaked almonds, toasted
1 cup fresh berries, or any fresh fruit of your choice
extra honey, to drizzle (optional)

1. Place rolled oats in a bowl. Pour over apple juice and lemon juice and stir to combine. Cover bowl with a plate and leave oats to soak for two hours, or overnight in the fridge.

2. Stir in grated apple, mashed banana, honey and yoghurt and mix well.

3. Spoon into serving bowls and scatter with toasted almonds and fresh berries. Drizzle with extra honey, if desired.

✱ **Kitchen savvy** . . . Use a plate instead of plastic wrap to cover the bowl. This will save you money and will also help save the planet from excess plastic waste. This is what our grandmothers did and we can learn a lot from their methods.

Toasted Almond Granola

Granola is a toasted version of muesli, and this one is particularly crunchy due to the crisp snap of the toasted almonds it contains. I've drastically cut the amount of sugar and added no extra fat to this mixture, so you will find it delightfully healthy but still big on flavour.

MAKES 18 SERVES DF | EF | WF | V

4 cups old-fashioned rolled oats
1 cup thread coconut
1 cup whole almonds
¼ cup flax seeds
¼ cup sesame seeds
2 tsp cinnamon

½ cup honey
2 tsp pure vanilla extract
1 cup dried fruit, such as raisins, Craisins, chopped pitted dates, figs or prunes (optional)

1. Preheat oven to 170 °C. Line a large oven pan with non-stick baking paper. Place rolled oats, coconut, almonds, seeds and cinnamon in a large bowl.
2. Warm honey with vanilla, either in a small saucepan or in a bowl in the microwave. Pour honey over oat mixture and stir to coat.
3. Spread mixture evenly over surface of prepared oven pan. Bake for 20 minutes, or until granola is toasted golden brown. Stir regularly so ingredients cook evenly and watch carefully, as mixture can brown quite quickly.
4. Remove pan from oven and stir in dried fruit, if desired. (Any dried fruit needs to be added once base mixture is toasted, as the natural sugar in the fruit tends to burn if toasted in the oven.)
5. Set granola aside to cool to room temperature, then transfer to an airtight container for storage. Serve with natural yoghurt and fresh, stewed, poached or baked fruit, such as rhubarb. Alternatively, serve with a dairy milk substitute, such as soy, rice or almond milk, if preferred.

Baked Rhubarb

This rhubarb holds its shape nicely, but if you want the rhubarb to fall apart, then simply bake for an extra 10 minutes.

SERVES 4   DF | EF | GF | WF | V

6 stalks rhubarb, trimmed and cut in 7-cm lengths – be sure to cut off any leafy parts
½ cup sugar

1. Preheat oven to 190 °C. Place rhubarb in a ceramic baking dish in a single layer and scatter with sugar.
2. Cover dish securely with foil. Bake for 30 minutes, or until rhubarb is tender but still holds its shape. Serve hot or cold.

* **Oats** . . . Oats are one of the very best ways to start the day. The right oats make all the difference – choose old-fashioned oats or steel-cut oats (not instant versions) because these are less processed, providing a great source of fibre to keep you feeling full longer and give sustained energy release. Oats are nutritious, containing protein and minerals, as well as antioxidants that can help lower cholesterol levels and boost the immune system.

* **Yoghurt** . . . Natural yoghurt is an excellent source of calcium and contains live active cultures and beneficial bacteria known as probiotics. Research shows that encouraging the growth of healthy bacteria in the digestive tract with probiotics may boost immunity, help the body absorb nutrients and decrease some digestive disorders. Check the label and be sure to buy yoghurt that contains live active bacteria.

Homemade Gluten–Free Muesli

This muesli is full of yummy things and makes for a great way to start the day. The quinoa and amaranth provide some natural protein, which is an important part of every balanced meal.

SERVES 12   DF | EF | GF | WF | V

- -

1 cup puffed rice
1 cup gluten–free corn flakes
1 cup walnut pieces (or almonds, if preferred)
½ cup puffed amaranth
½ cup puffed quinoa
½ cup thread coconut
½ cup raisins
½ cup dried Craisins
½ cup chopped dried apricots
½ cup sunflower seeds
¼ cup flax seeds

- -

1. Toss all ingredients together in a bowl to combine. Store in an airtight container.
2. Serve with fresh or poached fruit and milk of your choice, or with yoghurt.

*   Natural selection . . . Ingredients such as flax seeds, puffed amaranth and quinoa are readily available from health food stores and some supermarkets. Derived from the plant source, flax seed offers a vegetarian alternative containing omega-3 fatty acids. Also full of fibre, it has been determined in many studies that flax seed offers heart-healthy benefits.

Honey-Poached Summer Peaches

These pretty poached peaches also make a delightfully light dessert.

MAKES 4   DF | EF | GF | WF | V

- -

4 ripe but firm peaches
½ cup honey
1 cup raw sugar
4 cups cold filtered water
zest and juice of 1 lemon

- -

1. To peel peaches, make a light incision into peach skin, cutting around the centre of each peach. Plunge peaches into boiling water for 30–60 seconds, and then plunge into cold water. This will make the skins easy to remove (they should simply lift off) and discard.
2. Place honey, sugar, water and lemon zest and juice in a medium saucepan. Bring to the boil then turn down the heat and simmer for 5 minutes. Add the peaches to the pan. Place a piece of baking paper on top of the water to make sure the peaches are covered in liquid. Simmer for 10–15 minutes or until peaches are just tender.
3. Remove the peaches and liquid to a bowl to cool. Poached peaches last well for up to three days, if stored covered in the fridge. Serve with muesli and yoghurt, if desired.

Cinnamon Banana Porridge

This richly flavoured and warming porridge is a wonderful way to start a winter's day. Eating oats at breakfast can help us maintain a healthy weight thanks to the magic of fibre and water, which fill us up on fewer calories and then digest slowly so we feel satisfied between breakfast and lunch.

SERVES 4   EF | WF | V

- -

1½ cups old-fashioned rolled oats, or substitute quinoa flakes for a gluten-free version
4 cups cold filtered water
1 tsp cinnamon
¼ tsp salt
2 bananas, sliced
milk of choice, to serve
honey, to serve (optional)

- -

1. Place rolled oats or quinoa flakes, water, cinnamon and salt in a saucepan. Bring mixture to the boil, stirring to combine, and then turn down heat.

2. Simmer for 5 minutes, stirring regularly, until the mixture is thick. Stir the bananas in for the last minute of cooking.

3. Spoon porridge into bowls. Serve with milk of your choice and top with dried fruit compote or a drizzle of honey, if desired.

*   Kitchen savvy . . . If you don't want to deal with cleaning a dirty saucepan first thing in the morning then this porridge can easily be made in a bowl in the microwave. Simply mix the ingredients in a bowl, cover with a plate and microwave on high for 4 minutes. Add the banana, stir the mixture and microwave for another 2 minutes, or until the oats have softened and the mixture thickened.

Dried Fruit Compote

An interesting alternative way of serving this compote is to remove the cinnamon stick and vanilla pod and purée the fruit and syrup. This makes a rich fruity paste that is lovely with porridge or muesli.

SERVES 6–8   DF | EF | GF | WF | V

- -

1 cup dried figs
1 cup dried apricots
1 cup pitted prunes
1 vanilla bean, split in half lengthways
1 cinnamon stick
juice and pared rind of 1 lemon
juice of 1 orange
3 cups cold filtered water
⅓ cup honey

- -

1. Place all ingredients, except honey, in a medium saucepan and bring just to the boil. Turn down heat and simmer gently for 20 minutes until the fruit has softened and liquid is reduced.

2. Add honey and simmer for 5 minutes more or until remaining liquid is syrupy.

3. Remove to a bowl to cool. Refrigerate until ready to serve. Dried fruit compote will last well for up to one week if stored covered in the fridge.

*   Apricots . . . Organic dried apricots may not look quite as gorgeous as the bright orange versions, but this is because they have not been treated with chemical preservatives. So, while they may be slightly brownish in colour, organic dried apricots are better for you than their non-organic counterparts, not to mention super high in concentrated apricot flavour.

Oat Hotcakes with Hot Blueberry Sauce

Topped with hot blueberry sauce, these hotcakes are a pancake-lover's dream. It seems everyone loves hotcakes and these dairy-free and wheat-free breakfast delights are no exception (though it is important to note that oats do contain some gluten, so this is not a good recipe for those who follow a gluten-free diet).

SERVES 4   DF | WF | V

1½ cups old-fashioned
    rolled oats
¼ cup raw sugar
1¼ cups soy or rice milk
2 tbsp olive oil
1 egg, lightly beaten
¼ cup rice flour
¼ cup tapioca flour
1 tsp baking soda

1 tsp cream of tartar
½ tsp cinnamon
¼ tsp salt
extra soy or rice milk,
    if required
olive oil, for frying
Hot blueberry sauce (recipe
    follows)

1. Place rolled oats and sugar in a bowl, cover with milk and set aside to soak for 10 minutes. Add oil and egg and stir to combine.

2. Add sifted flours, baking soda, cream of tartar, cinnamon and salt and stir to form a smooth batter. Add 1–2 tablespoons extra milk to thin, if necessary.

3. In a large frying-pan set over medium heat, cook big spoonfuls of mixture in a little oil for 2 minutes on each side, turning once, until golden brown. You will have 12 small hotcakes.

4. This will need to be done in batches, so keep hotcakes warm in a moderate oven until you have cooked them all. Serve with hot blueberry sauce.

❋   Good idea . . . For early morning ease, or if you're feeding a crowd, this hotcake batter can be prepared the night before and tossed to order when desired. Often the first hotcake made isn't the best and may need to be discarded. Learn from this test run and make adjustments to the heat of the pan so that hotcakes cook through without becoming too dark on the outside.

Hot Blueberry Sauce

Hot blueberry sauce is naturally good with hotcakes or pancakes of any kind but also makes a delicious topping to other goodies, such as porridge, muesli and waffles.

MAKES 1½ CUPS   DF | EF | GF | WF | V

1½ cups blueberries (fresh or frozen)
⅓ cup honey
1 tbsp cold filtered water

1. Combine the blueberries, honey and water in a saucepan and bring just to the boil, then remove from the heat.
2. Serve hot, spooned over a stack of hotcakes.

Hot Apricot Breakfast Scones

Although these fruity scones can be made with ordinary flour, I make them with spelt flour, because spelt flour is easier for the body to digest. If necessary, they can also be made with gluten-free flour mix, though this will make them a bit heavier. I have also suggested using fruit purée instead of milk, which not only makes these scones dairy-free, but appealingly fruity flavoured, as well.

MAKES 12   DF | EF

- -

3½ cups spelt flour (or substitute all-purpose flour or
   gluten-free flour mix, as preferred)
3½ tsp gluten-free baking powder
pinch of salt
410-g can apricots in natural juice
3 tbsp light olive oil
1 tsp pure vanilla extract
extra flour, for dusting
Low-sugar berry jam, to serve (see page 71)

- -

1. Preheat oven to 210 °C. Line a baking sheet with baking paper. Sift flour, baking powder and salt into a large mixing bowl and make a well in the centre.

2. Purée apricots and their juice. You should end up with 1¾ cups of purée. If necessary, make up any difference by adding a little water.

3. Pour purée into the well, add oil and vanilla, and then, using a dinner knife, mix together to just combine. Turn the mixture out onto a lightly floured work surface. Knead very briefly and lightly to bring together into a moist dough.

4. Press the dough into a 3-cm thick block. Cut into 12 squares and place on the prepared baking sheet.

5. Bake for 15 minutes or until puffed and golden brown. Cut in half and serve hot, topped with a good dollop of berry jam.

Peach and Berry Smoothies

These layered smoothies look enticing and make a nutritious and revitalising breakfast or brunch drink.

SERVES 4   EF | GF | WF

- -

3 ripe peaches, coarsely chopped with stones removed
1 cup plain unsweetened yoghurt
1 tbsp LSA (see note, below)
6 tbsp liquid honey
2 cups mixed berries (fresh or frozen)
½ cup cranberry juice

- -

1. Place chopped peaches, yoghurt, LSA and 3 tablespoons of the honey in a blender and process to purée. Chill mixture in fridge. Rinse out blender.

2. Place berries, cranberry juice and remaining honey in blender and process to purée. Chill mixture separately in fridge.

3. Divide berry mixture between four tall glasses, then spoon some peach mixture on top.

✱   **LSA** . . . A nutritious blend of flax seeds, sunflower kernels and whole almonds ground together, you can either buy LSA from health stores or make a batch yourself, using equal parts of each ingredient. LSA contains fibre, protein and omega-3 fatty acids, so is a great addition to everyday meals. Sprinkle 1–2 tablespoons over your cereal each morning, mix into muffins or cakes, or add to smoothies like this one.

✱   **My advice** . . . For super scones, try to work the mixture as little as possible once the wet ingredients have been added to the dry ingredients to ensure the finished scones turn out soft and light.

Scrambled Eggs with Tomatoes

SERVES 2   GF | WF

2 medium tomatoes, seeds and cores removed
4 eggs
¼ cup cream (or substitute soy or rice milk)
salt and freshly ground black pepper
1 tbsp olive oil or butter
1 tbsp chopped fresh parsley

1. Cut tomato flesh into strips. Break eggs into a bowl, add cream and beat lightly to combine. Stir in the strips of tomato and season with salt and pepper.
2. Heat a saucepan and add oil or butter to melt. Pour in egg mixture and cook over medium heat. As the egg sets around the edges, use a wooden spoon to draw the set mixture into the centre of the pan.
3. Continue in this way until all the egg mixture is just set. Take care not to overcook the scramble or it will be dry and crumbly.
4. The trick is to remove scramble from pan when still a little underdone, as it will continue to cook and set on the down-heat. Scatter with parsley and serve with sourdough or gluten-free toast.

Turkish Eggs

SERVES 2   DF

2 tbsp olive oil
2 cloves garlic, finely sliced
2–4 eggs
3 tbsp lemon juice
salt and freshly ground black pepper
Turkish flatbread, toasted (or substitute pita bread)
½ tsp freshly ground cumin seeds
fresh mint leaves, torn

1. Heat oil in a large frying-pan set over medium–low heat. Add garlic and cook for 30 seconds until golden brown.
2. Break eggs (allowing 1–2 per person) into the pan and fry gently until just set, adding lemon juice towards the end of cooking.
3. Season eggs with salt and pepper and serve on toasted Turkish bread. Sprinkle each dish with a good pinch of cumin and scatter with torn mint leaves.

Baked Eggs with Smoked Fish and Chives

SERVES 4   DF | GF | WF

olive oil spray
8 organic or free-range eggs
1 cup flaked smoked fish of your choice, such as tuna or salmon
½ cup cherry tomatoes, halved
salt and freshly ground black pepper
2 tbsp chopped fresh chives
wholegrain or gluten-free toast, to serve

1. Preheat oven to 180 °C. Spray four ovenproof ramekins or small ovenproof dishes with olive oil.
2. Break two eggs into each ramekin. Add some flaked smoked fish to each ramekin, top with a few cherry tomato halves and season with salt and pepper.
3. Cover ramekins with foil and place on an oven tray. Bake for 30 minutes or until eggs are just soft set (or 5 minutes longer for hard-cooked egg yolks).
4. Remove ramekins from oven, remove foil and sprinkle with chives. Serve immediately, with toast on the side.

Poached Eggs with Pan-Fried Spinach

SERVES 2   DF

1 tbsp white wine vinegar
4 really fresh eggs
2 tbsp olive oil
150 g baby spinach leaves
salt and freshly ground black pepper
bagels or toast, to serve

1. Half-fill a wide saucepan with water and bring to a rolling boil. Stir in vinegar (this helps the egg whites to set and the eggs keep their shape). Stir water to create a nice swirling motion.
2. Break eggs into tea cups and then slip them, one at a time, into the water. Lower heat so water is gently bubbling and poach eggs for 2–3 minutes for soft yolks.
3. While eggs are poaching, heat oil in a small frying-pan. Add spinach and stir-fry quickly to wilt. Season with salt and pepper.
4. Arrange spinach on hot buttered bagels, or toast of your choice, and place the poached eggs on top.

✱ **Natural selection** . . . The fresher the egg, the higher its nutritional value. For the best poached eggs, use eggs that are extremely fresh, as these will hold their shape better and won't break up in the poaching water.

Kitchen Garden

pots of herbs and homegrown fruit and vegetables

* **Plant a patch**, pot or container and reap more rewards than you can imagine. Fostering an edible garden can be both enjoyable and beneficial. Gardening can be good exercise for starters, and there's much satisfaction to be gained from cooking and eating freshly picked produce you have grown yourself. Fruits and vegetables just seem to taste better when you have invested your time into coaxing these food crops from the earth. Plus, there's no time wasted getting fresh produce from plant to plate, making homegrown produce a healthier way to eat.

Ratatouille

This classic French dish is one of my most favourite meals. More than just a chunky vegetable stew, when properly cooked, ratatouille takes on a melt-in-the-mouth dimension and all the flavours mingle together in the most appealing way.

SERVES 4   DF | EF | GF | WF | V

olive oil
1 large onion, chopped
2 red capsicums, cut into chunks
2 cloves garlic, chopped
1 medium eggplant, cubed
3–4 small courgettes, thickly sliced

4 large tomatoes, coarsely chopped (or substitute 400-g can chopped organic tomatoes)
salt and freshly ground black pepper
2 tbsp torn fresh basil leaves

1. In a large heavy-based casserole dish or saucepan, heat 2 tablespoons olive oil over medium heat. Add onion and capsicums and cook, stirring often, for 8–10 minutes until softened and lightly browned.

2. Add garlic and cook for 1 minute more. Remove vegetables to one side, reserving any oil in the pan. Add eggplant to pan, with a little more oil, and cook, tossing often, to lightly brown all over.

3. Remove eggplant to one side and add courgettes to pan, tossing to lightly brown. Return all vegetables to pan.

4. Stir in tomatoes and any juice. Cover and simmer for 20 minutes, stirring occasionally until vegetables are tender. Check and adjust seasoning with salt and pepper. Serve scattered with torn basil leaves.

✱   My advice . . . The proportions of ratatouille can be easily varied, depending on the produce at hand. This recipe is close to the classical method where the vegetables are first browned separately and then cooked together. However, if you're short on time, I find that all the vegetables can be oven-roasted in one big tray first and then cooked in the pan with the tomatoes.

Vegetable Terrine

Terrines are classic, rustic French dishes that have been popular for generations. This vegetable terrine not only delights the eye with its layers of colour, but is perfect for sharing with friends in a convivial way.

SERVES 8 GF | WF

500 g all-purpose potatoes, peeled
200 g green beans, trimmed
2 carrots, peeled and cut into long, 1-cm
  thick strips

2 roasted red capsicums, cut into thick strips
salt and freshly ground black pepper
4 small eggs, lightly beaten
⅓ cup cream

1. Preheat oven to 150 °C. Grease a 1.5-litre-capacity loaf tin and line with non-stick baking paper, leaving an overhang on all sides. Cook potatoes whole in boiling, salted water for 15 minutes or until just tender. Drain well and, when cool enough to handle, cut into 1-cm thick slices.

2. At the same time, blanch beans and carrot strips in boiling water for 1 minute then drain well and set aside to cool. Arrange half the potatoes over the base of the prepared tin. Cover with a layer of half the capsicums.

3. Arrange half the beans and all the carrots over top and then remaining beans and sliced capsicums, seasoning between layers. Top with remaining potato slices.

4. In a bowl, lightly whisk together eggs and cream. Pour mixture in small amounts into terrine until liquid sinks in between layers and tin is full. Cover tin with foil and bake for 60 minutes or until set.

5. Leave terrine in tin for 20 minutes to cool and become firm, then invert tin to remove terrine. Slice with a sharp knife and serve warm or cold.

✱ **Natural selection** . . . Any seasonal garden vegetables can be substituted for the ones listed in this recipe. Try springtime asparagus in place of green beans or broccoli florets in winter. Baby leeks work well, too, as do kumara in place of the ordinary potatoes.

Cherry Tomato Risotto with Summer Basil Pesto

Cherry tomatoes are probably the easiest tomatoes of all to grow. A single plant can produce a good harvest that are delicious to eat like sweets or to use in salads and cooked dishes. The natural sweet-sour tang of tomatoes makes a lighter flavoured risotto — perfect for a refreshing summery meal.

SERVES 4 EF | GF | WF

- 4 cups liquid vegetable or chicken stock, as preferred
- 2 tbsp tomato paste
- 2 tbsp olive oil
- 2 cloves garlic, crushed
- I onion, peeled and finely diced
- I½ cups Italian risotto rice, such as carnaroli, vialone nano or arborio
- ½ cup dry white wine
- I½ cups cherry tomatoes
- salt and freshly ground black pepper
- I tbsp butter or olive oil
- extra hot stock, if necessary
- 4 tbsp Summer basil pesto (recipe follows)
- shaved fresh Parmesan or pecorino

I. Heat stock and tomato paste in a small saucepan. Heat a large heavy-based pan, add oil, garlic and onion and cook over a medium–low heat for 8 minutes to soften but not brown.

2. Add rice and stir for 2 minutes to toast but not brown. Add wine and stir until almost completely evaporated.

3. Add one cup of hot stock to the rice and stir well over medium heat. When rice has absorbed liquid, add another cup of stock. Continue to stir and keep adding hot stock until all absorbed — after I5–20 minutes the rice should be *al dente* (tender to the bite) and surrounded by a creamy sauce.

4. Stir in cherry tomatoes and season with salt and pepper to taste. Cover the pan and leave to steam for 5 minutes. Stir in the butter and/or a little more hot stock just before serving to give a creamy consistency.

5. Serve in bowls topped with a good dollop of summer basil pesto and some shaved Parmesan or pecorino, as desired.

Summer Basil Pesto

Rich in flavour and nutrients, herbs must be the easiest edible plants of all to grow, plus herbs grow well in pots and very small spaces.

MAKES 1¼ CUPS   EF | GF | WF

- 1 clove garlic, peeled
- 1 cup firmly packed basil leaves
- ¼ cup grated fresh Parmesan
- ¼ cup pine nuts, toasted
- ½ cup extra virgin olive oil
- salt and freshly ground black pepper

1. Place garlic and basil in the bowl of a food processor and pulse to chop. Add Parmesan and pine nuts and process to coarsely grind.
2. With the motor running, add oil through the feed tube in a thin stream, processing until amalgamated into a thick paste. Season with salt and pepper to taste.
3. Store pesto covered with a film of olive oil on the surface to prevent discolouration.

* **Italian risotto rice** . . . To make a good risotto, you need a special kind of short-grain rice specifically used for making traditional Italian risotto. This rice has the ability to absorb liquid (stock) while letting out starch and still retaining its shape, which makes for the perfect creamy risotto consistency. Look for carnaroli, vialone nano or arborio risotto rice in your favourite deli or specialty food store.

Silver Beet, Leek and Feta Pies

Vegetable pies are a recurring culinary theme throughout the Mediterranean region where seasonal produce, local cheeses and herbs, often bound with eggs, are packed into dough and baked until golden. These rustic pies are a lighter version of the typical Greek spinach and feta spanakopita, and are a delicious way to work more vegetables into your diet.

SERVES 4

1 tbsp olive oil
1 leek, washed, trimmed and finely sliced
2 cloves garlic, finely chopped
500 g silver beet, washed
½ cup fresh whole-wheat breadcrumbs
250 g ricotta cheese

150 g feta, crumbled
3 large eggs, lightly beaten
salt and freshly ground black pepper
150 g filo pastry sheets
olive oil spray

1. Preheat oven to 190 °C. Grease four individual ovenproof pie dishes or ramekins. Heat oil in a large frying-pan. Add sliced leek and cook for 5 minutes over medium heat until softened but not browned. Add garlic and cook for 1 minute more.

2. Remove stems and main thick vein from silver beet and coarsely shred the green leaves. Add shredded silver beet to pan and stir-fry over fairly high heat to drive off excess moisture. Transfer mixture to a large bowl to cool.

3. Add breadcrumbs, ricotta and feta cheese to the cooled silver beet. Stir in the beaten eggs and season well with salt and pepper, mixing well to combine. Spoon the mixture into the prepared dishes and press with the back of a spoon to smooth the surface.

4. Cut the roll of filo pastry sheets into 2-cm thick sections. Toss the sliced filo on a board to separate into ribbons. Completely cover silver beet mixture in each dish with a pile of filo ribbons and spray lightly with oil.

5. Bake pies for 30–35 minutes or until filling is set and filo pastry is golden brown.

✳ Ricotta . . . A fresh cheese made from milk whey, ricotta is white with a grainy, fine-crumb texture and a delicate, creamy, slightly sweet taste. Ricotta is naturally lower in fat and salt than other types of fresh cheese, so is a healthy choice for baking. Ricotta is readily available from supermarkets and delis.

Beetroot and Goat's Cheese Salad with Pine Nut Dressing

Beetroot, with all its healthful qualities, is one of the most common vegetables grown by home gardeners. It's a popular choice because it is relatively easy to grow and can also be grown successfully in containers. Both the leaves and the roots are edible and both contain many important dietary nutrients.

SERVES 4–6   EF | GF | WF

800 g small beetroot, scrubbed
salt
100 g rocket leaves
¼ cup currants
¼ cup pine nuts, toasted

100 g soft goat's cheese, crumbled
Pine nut dressing (recipe follows)
1 tbsp chopped fresh mint

1. Cook beetroot whole, covered in plenty of boiling, salted water for 30–40 minutes, depending on size, until tender when skewered with the point of a sharp knife. Drain and set aside to cool.

2. Once cool enough to handle, the skins will simply slip off. Remove the skins from the beetroot and discard. Cut the beetroot into wedges.

3. Arrange the rocket on a serving platter. Scatter with the beetroot wedges, currants, pine nuts and crumbled goat's cheese. Serve drizzled with the pine nut dressing and scattered with chopped fresh mint.

✴ **Beetroot** . . . Beetroot is packed full of beneficial vitamins, minerals and fibre. Among its many attributes, beetroot contains the minerals magnesium and silica, both of which help the body absorb calcium effectively to help maintain healthy bones. Beetroot has cholesterol-lowering capabilities and antioxidants that help to cleanse the liver and keep it functioning properly.

✴ **Kitchen savvy** . . . To toast seeds or nuts, heat the oven to 180 °C. Place the seeds or nuts in a small frying-pan with a heatproof handle or in a small oven pan and place in the oven for approximately 10 minutes, stirring once during cooking, until golden brown. Watch carefully so they don't burn, as seeds and nuts tend to brown suddenly. Remove to cool.

Pine Nut Dressing

Not nuts at all but the seeds from certain species of pine, pine nuts are a small but power-packed source of protein, fibre, iron, magnesium and antioxidants. High in good fats (monounsaturated fats, like olive oil), which can help reduce unhealthy cholesterol levels, pine nuts also contain pinoleic acid, which is known to be an appetite suppressant.

MAKES ⅔ CUP   DF | EF | GF | WF

½ cup pine nuts, toasted
1 tbsp wholegrain mustard
2 tbsp apple cider vinegar
¼ cup extra virgin olive oil
salt and freshly ground black pepper

1. Combine pine nuts, mustard, vinegar and oil in the bowl of a small food processor and process to combine into a coarse-textured dressing. Alternatively, pound ingredients in a mortar with a pestle to make a paste.
2. Season with salt and pepper to taste.

Glorious Green Soup

Like most soups, this one will last well for several days if covered and stored in the fridge. In fact, soups generally improve with keeping for a day or two, as the flavours mature and meld together. The addition of cream cheese gives this soup a wonderful texture and slightly sour, cheesy taste. However, this ingredient can be omitted if a dairy-free soup is preferred.

SERVES 6–8   EF | GF | WF

2 tbsp olive oil
1 leek, trimmed and sliced
2 sticks celery, chopped
500 g (2 large) mashing
  potatoes, peeled and chopped
6 cups vegetable cooking water
  or cold filtered water
1 small head broccoli, coarsely
  chopped
500 g spinach, well washed with
  stems removed

¼ cup fresh parsley leaves
½ cup low-fat cream cheese
  (optional)
¼ tsp freshly grated nutmeg
salt and freshly ground black
  pepper
fresh soft herbs, such as parsley
  or basil, to garnish

1. Heat oil in a large, heavy-based saucepan. Add leek and celery and cook over medium heat for 10 minutes to soften but not brown.

2. Add potatoes and pour on the water. Bring to the boil, then turn down heat and simmer gently for 10 minutes, or until potatoes are tender.

3. Add broccoli and simmer for 2 minutes. Add spinach and parsley and cook for 2 minutes more, so that the leaves wilt but remain bright green.

4. Purée the mixture in batches in a blender or food processor, incorporating the cream cheese as you blend, if desired. Season with nutmeg and salt and pepper to taste. Garnish with herbs and serve with quesadillas on the side.

✳ My advice . . . Save vegetable cooking water to use as a simple stock base for soups, as it contains vitamins, minerals and flavours from the vegetables.

Quesadillas

Quesadillas are small Mexican turnovers made by sandwiching tortillas together with a stuffing and then lightly pan-frying them until crisp and golden.

MAKES 24 WEDGES   DF | EF | V

½ cup sun-dried tomatoes in olive oil
1 clove garlic, chopped
6 soft flour tortillas
olive oil spray

1. Combine sun-dried tomatoes, including any oil, and garlic in a mini food processor and process to form a thick paste.
2. Lay three tortillas on a bench. Spread each with sun-dried tomato paste. Sandwich together with remaining tortillas.
3. Heat a frying-pan and lightly spray with oil. Place one tortilla sandwich in the pan at a time to toast for 2 minutes on each side or until golden brown and crisp. Remove to a board and cut each quesadilla into 8 wedges. Serve warm.

Ginger, Pear and Carrot Chutney

With a great colour, flavour and texture, this winter chutney works well on sandwiches, with strong cheeses, or enjoy it simply as a dip with crusty bread.

MAKES 5 CUPS   DF | EF | GF | WF | V

750 g (4–5 medium-sized) pears, peeled, cored and diced
2 onions, finely diced
¾ cup sultanas
1 tbsp curry powder
1 tbsp grated fresh ginger

1 tsp mustard seeds
1½ cups cider vinegar
1½ cups raw sugar
2 tsp salt
400 g (3–4 medium-sized) carrots, peeled and coarsely grated

1. Place all ingredients, except carrots, in a saucepan and bring to the boil, stirring until the sugar dissolves.
2. Turn down heat and simmer hard for 30 minutes, then stir in grated carrots. Simmer more gently for another 30 minutes, or until liquid is reduced and the mixture is thick.
3. Spoon chutney into sterilised jars and seal well (see note below). Store in a cool dark place for at least 2 weeks for the flavours to mature before eating.

✻ Kitchen savvy . . . Sterilising jars is important to protect your preserves from spoiling. To do this, wash jars well in hot soapy water, then rinse and place them in an oven preheated to 160 °C for 20 minutes. Ladle hot chutney into hot jars and seal immediately. Stored and sealed correctly, chutney will last for at least 12 months. Chutney is best kept in the fridge after opening. A high percentage of vinegar, sugar and salt is necessary for the preservation of the chutney, and for flavour. However, the amount of these ingredients consumed at any one time is minimal, considering only a small spoonful of chutney is needed to add a flavour boost to any particular meal.

Ginger, pear
& carrot
chutney

Roast Cauliflower Salad

SERVES 6, AS A SIDE DISH   DF | EF | GF | WF | V

1 large cauliflower
¼ cup olive oil
4 cloves garlic, crushed
salt and freshly ground black pepper
4 tbsp chopped fresh parsley
⅓ cup pine nuts, lightly toasted

1. Preheat oven to 170 °C. Cut cauliflower into small even-sized florets and place in a large oven pan lined with non-stick baking paper.
2. Combine oil and garlic and drizzle over cauliflower. Season with salt and pepper and toss well to coat.
3. Roast cauliflower for 30 minutes, or until golden brown, stirring occasionally to allow for even browning.
4. Serve scattered with parsley and pine nuts. This recipe can be served hot as a vegetable side dish or cold as a tasty salad.

Garden Tomato Salad

SERVES 4, AS A SIDE DISH   DF | EF | GF | WF | V

6 large vine-ripened tomatoes
1 cup cherry tomatoes
100 g rocket leaves, coarsely chopped
¼ cup chopped parsley
3 spring onions, finely sliced
salt and freshly ground black pepper
1 clove garlic, crushed
1 tbsp pomegranate molasses
3 tbsp extra virgin olive oil

1. Cut large tomatoes into chunks, removing the cores.
2. Place in a bowl with the cherry tomatoes, rocket, parsley and spring onions. Season with salt and pepper and toss well.
3. Make a dressing by placing the garlic, pomegranate molasses and oil in a small bowl. Whisk to combine then drizzle the dressing over the salad and toss well to coat.

Pesto Potato Salad

SERVES 6, AS A SIDE DISH   GF | WF | EF

1 kg baby salad potatoes
salt and freshly ground black pepper
⅓ cup Summer basil pesto (see page 39)
3 tbsp extra virgin olive oil
100 g feta, crumbled
¼ cup torn fresh basil leaves, to garnish

1. Cook potatoes in plenty of boiling, salted water for
10 minutes, or until just tender.
2. Drain well then cut any larger potatoes in half. Place
potatoes in a serving bowl to cool.
3. Make a dressing by placing pesto and oil in a small bowl
and whisking to combine. Drizzle dressing over potatoes, add
salt and pepper to taste and toss well to coat.
4. Serve scattered with feta and fresh basil.

Lebanese Cucumber and Radish Salad

SERVES 4, AS A SIDE DISH   DF | EF | GF | WF | V

2 Lebanese cucumbers, thinly sliced
2 small carrots, thinly sliced
1 bunch radishes, thinly sliced
juice of 1 lemon
3–4 tbsp extra virgin olive oil
salt and freshly ground black pepper
¼ cup torn fresh mint leaves, to garnish

1. Prepare all salad vegetables and place in a large bowl.
2. Drizzle with lemon juice and oil, season with salt and
pepper and toss well.
3. Serve scattered with torn fresh mint.

✳ **Fresh herbs** . . . Fresh herbs contain essential
oils that add healthy goodness and a tasty zing
to any dish. Try parsley, fennel or dill with seafood;
coriander, Thai basil or mint in Asian-style dishes;
and basil, thyme, oregano, sage or rosemary with
Mediterranean recipes.

Start a Kitchen Garden

Starting your own edible garden is much easier than you might imagine and the rewards can be enormous. Any avid gardener will agree that homegrown produce simply tastes better. Plus, if you use organic principles in your garden, then the fruits of your labour are bound to be better for you, too. Gathering fruits and vegetables that you have nurtured can provide a huge sense of pleasure. And, of course, you get to cook and eat them at their freshest and most nutritious.

There are other benefits, too. Communing with nature can be very relaxing and a garden full of greens can form a peaceful refuge, full of pleasant, revitalising herbal perfumes. Digging and moving garden plants, compost and soil can be a good exercise workout, too, as you renew your relationship with nature.

The Right Space
You don't actually need a huge amount of space to set up a kitchen garden, though it is important to find a nice sheltered, sunny spot and to prepare the soil well. With access to only a small patch of ground, a patio, balcony or deck and some containers, you can feed yourself and others.

I have a small garden and I don't claim to be an expert by any means, but it seems to me that the more effort you put into gardening, the more rewards you will reap. If you find yourself becoming serious about gardening, then the best place to get essential information is from a good gardening manual. I also suggest making friends with your local gardening supplier who will be able to answer your questions as they pop up.

However big or small, I really want to encourage you to start a kitchen garden of some sort, because it's a very healthy, tasty and fun pastime for anyone who likes to cook.

Herbs, Pots and Planters
No matter where I've lived, the first thing I've always done when I've moved into a new home is plant fresh herbs. Herbs are particularly easy to grow and harvest rich rewards, especially, of course, if you're a passionate cook. Place potted herbal plants near the kitchen or by a barbecue area, so you can have them close at hand for cooking and garnishing food. You'll find fresh herbs are an invaluable asset to your cooking for the flavour and concentrated goodness they impart.

Herbs flourish happily in small pots, too, so even apartment dwellers or those with very little space can grow pots of herbs on the windowsill, or in containers set on a balcony. It's also possible to plant some fruits and vegetables in containers, which make for easy-access tending and harvesting. I find that tomatoes, cherry tomatoes, strawberries, salad greens, spinach and even carrots, beets and chilli peppers all work well in containers. I also have both a lemon and a lime tree in large pots and these produce good fruit, though not in large amounts.

Seasonal Plants
As fruits and vegetables are seasonal plants, it's important to realise that different plants do better at different times of the year and they must be planted at the right time to get the best results. It is possible to simply give plants a go and learn from trial and error. But if you want to get into gardening in a big way, then I'd check with your local gardening guru, or consult a garden manual for a seasonal guide to growing your own produce.

As an example, salad greens are an excellent beginner gardener's choice for summer. I like to plant a variety of different lettuces and then pick mixed fresh leaves, as they come through. Spinach and silver beet are great throughout the winter months — simply pick off a few leaves, as you need them. Picking your own means there's less time from plant to plate, so you get the maximum benefit of available nutrients.

"No matter where I've lived, the first thing I've always done when I've moved into a new home is plant fresh herbs. Herbs are particularly easy to grow and harvest rich rewards, especially, of course, if you're a passionate cook."

Organics and Composting

Another bonus of having your own edible garden is that you have control over gardening practices, such as the type of plant food used and methods of pest reduction. Organic gardening methods are better for your health and better for the planet.

The central philosophy of organic gardening is to work with nature, not against it. Companion planting is one clever organic practice. This is when plants are grown together with other species that naturally keep pests away, or with plants that attract natural pest predators, such as birds. Make and use natural organic compost to keep your garden soil healthy and fertile, as quality soil will establish stronger plants that are naturally more resistant to disease and pests.

The most important thing to know when starting a compost heap is that it needs layers to be successful. Start by layering kitchen waste such as fruit and vegetable peelings and coffee grounds along with garden waste like grass clippings and leaves. Top this with some handfuls of soil and add some dry stuff like leaves and even paper to absorb excess moisture. Continue these layers, keeping it moist but never too wet, turn the pile once in a while, and nature will do the rest. Take care not to add any kitchen scraps of meat or fat to the compost heap, as these can ruin the results and attract rodents, cats and dogs.

Watering Plants

Water is, of course, important to the life of your edible plants and to the production of healthy fruits and vegetables. To be eco-friendly, collect rain water in recycled buckets to supplement your local supply and use a watering can instead of a hose to minimise waste. To water plants effectively, do so either in the morning or evening to avoid the direct heat of the sun. Remember that pots and containers need to be watered more frequently, as these dry out quickly.

Pass it On

If you have children, teaching them about gardening and letting them experience this form of self-sufficiency can be very rewarding for the whole family. I vividly remember as a child being given a little corner patch of my father's garden so I could grow my own plants. Because of this, I was, and still am, very fond of parsley, which grows effortlessly but adds such concentrated flavour and goodness to so many dishes. I also found radishes fun to grow, even though eating them was an acquired taste, for some. My grandmother introduced me to cherry tomato plants and their memorable harvests of tiny gems, as sweet as small red candies. My childhood attempts at gardening were pretty simple but the experience was invaluable and the pleasure has stayed with me all this time. And this is why I still keep up an edible garden today.

Gardening can teach your children about the different seasons as they experience the wonderful anticipation of seasonal crops, such as the super tasty strawberries of summer. Caring for plants teaches children new skills and gives them responsibility, respect and appreciation for the environment. Children can also learn about healthy eating through knowing where food comes from. If you can make this an everyday part of their lives, and make it fun, then they will take these skills and knowledge into their future and live better lives.

ORGANIC
BLUEBERRIES
grown in New Zealand

Superfoods

nutrient-rich, high-antioxidant foods

* **We all know** we must eat a wide variety of fresh, natural foods daily, as no single food can give the body everything it needs. However, it seems some foods contain more than their share of nutrients, antioxidants and health-giving properties – that's why they've been given the popular name: superfoods. It makes good sense to eat more of these particularly potent, natural foods that can boost our immune systems and help us reach optimum health. The good news is that these seemingly extraordinary foods are surprisingly ordinary and commonly available, so it's easy to find, cook and enjoy superfoods every day.

Avocado with Smoked Salmon and Bean Salad

Adding avocados to your diet is an excellent nutritional choice, as they contain high levels of vitamins and minerals for good health. Avocados and avocado oil make healthy substitutes for foods rich in saturated fats (which contain cholesterol). For an alternative and more casual presentation of this salad, slice the avocados and simply toss with all the other ingredients.

SERVES 4   DF | EF | GF | WF

I medium fennel bulb (or substitute 2 stalks celery, if preferred)
juice of 1 lemon
400-g can white cannellini beans
I clove garlic, crushed
2 spring onions, finely sliced
¼ cup chopped fresh parsley

¼ cup salted capers, rinsed and drained
2 tbsp extra virgin olive oil
salt and freshly ground black pepper
2 ripe avocados
100 g sliced cold smoked salmon
I lemon, cut into wedges, to serve

1. Finely slice fennel bulb and combine with half the lemon juice to stop it from discolouring.

2. Rinse and drain beans and place in a bowl with the garlic, spring onions, parsley, capers, oil and prepared fennel. Season with salt and pepper to taste and toss well.

3. Halve the avocados and remove the stones. Brush the cut surfaces of the avocados with the remaining lemon juice to prevent the avocados browning.

4. Spoon some bean salad into the cavity of each avocado half and arrange a slice of smoked salmon on top. Serve with lemon wedges on the side, to squeeze over the salad.

* Beans . . . Beans and other legumes (dried pulses) are rich in nutrients and high in protein and fibre, which puts them on the list of superfoods. A high-fibre intake helps you maintain healthy cholesterol and blood-sugar levels. Plus, fibre helps you feel full for longer and provides a source of sustained energy. Whole grains, fruit and vegetables are also good sources of fibre.

Broccoli Pasta Sauce

This tasty, nutrient-rich, bright green, classic Italian pasta sauce is traditionally made with orecchiette pasta but you can use any pasta you fancy, including whole-wheat pasta, or even gluten-free pasta, if required.

SERVES 4   EF

400 g quality pasta shapes, such as penne
1 head broccoli
¼ cup olive oil
3 cloves garlic, chopped
¼ tsp chilli flakes

juice of ½ lemon
salt and freshly ground black pepper
freshly shaved Parmesan or pecorino
 (optional)

1. Cook pasta in plenty of boiling, salted water for 8–10 minutes, or according to packet instructions, until *al dente* (just tender to the bite). Drain well and reserve one third of a cup of the cooking liquid.

2. Coarsely chop broccoli florets. Remove the fibrous exterior of the broccoli stem and coarsely chop.

3. Heat oil in a heavy-based pan, add garlic and chilli flakes and cook for 30 seconds over medium heat. Add broccoli, toss and stir-fry for 2–3 minutes. Add reserved pasta cooking liquid and continue to cook, tossing regularly until broccoli is tender to the bite.

4. Add drained pasta and toss well to coat with the sauce. Squeeze over lemon juice and season with salt and pepper to taste. Serve immediately topped with shaved Parmesan or pecorino, if desired.

* Broccoli . . . Broccoli and other dark green vegetables such as silver beet, kale and bok choy are packed with vitamins A and C, iron, calcium and other plant-based nutrients. These vegetables are also high in fibre (so they are filling) and low in calories, making them good foods to help keep your heart healthy and your waistline slim.

Chicken with Forty Cloves of Garlic

Tasty chicken dishes like this one are perennial favourites. Containing masses of garlic, this dish not only tastes fantastic, it also has the ability to ward off minor ills, and possibly vampires too, if necessary. Buying and portioning a whole chicken yourself can work out to be more economical than purchasing pre-cut pieces, and this way there's no wastage.

SERVES 6–8   DF | EF | GF | WF

1.5 kg organic or free-range chicken
1 cup dry white wine, such as a Sauvignon Blanc
3 tbsp extra virgin olive oil
salt and freshly ground black pepper

3 whole heads of garlic (approximately 40 cloves), cloves separated but not peeled
¼ cup fresh herbs, such as tarragon, oregano, thyme

1. Preheat oven to 190 °C. Cut chicken into 8 portions, trimming off any fat. Rinse portions well and pat dry with paper towels. Place chicken portions in an oven pan.
2. Pour wine over chicken, then drizzle with oil and season well with salt and pepper. Place in oven to roast for 25 minutes. Baste once or twice during cooking.
3. Lightly smash garlic cloves with the side of a heavy chef's knife, leaving the skin on. Scatter garlic over chicken in the pan and then continue roasting for a further 25–30 minutes, or until the chicken tests cooked. The chicken is cooked when a sharp knife is inserted into the thickest part of the thigh, close to the bone, and the juices run clear.
4. Transfer chicken pieces to a serving platter. Taste the pan juice and adjust the seasoning with salt and pepper, if necessary, then spoon the sauce over the chicken. Scatter with fresh herbs and serve.

* **Garlic** . . . The natural antibacterial and antifungal properties of garlic are known to boost our immune systems. However, in order for these benefits to become available to us, the garlic must first be chopped or crushed, as allicin, the key immune-boosting ingredient, only forms when exposed to air.

Sesame Salmon with Sweet and Sour Chilli Dressing

I love this hot, sweet, sour and salty dressing with salmon, as it cuts through the natural richness of the salmon flesh to complement it beautifully. I recommend cooking salmon with the skin on as the skin acts as a protective layer, holding in succulence and flavour. If you prefer not to eat the skin, then simply remove this after cooking and before serving.

SERVES 4   DF | EF

4 x 150-g portions extremely fresh salmon fillet, with the skin on
½ cup sesame seeds
light olive oil

¼ cup fresh coriander leaves, to garnish
1 cup Sweet and sour chilli dressing (recipe follows)
lime halves, to serve

I. Remove pin bones from salmon with tweezers, or get your fishmonger to do this for you.

2. Spread sesame seeds out on a plate. Press salmon, flesh-side down, in sesame seeds to coat.

3. Heat a little oil in a large frying-pan. Add the salmon to the pan, flesh-side down, and cook over medium heat for 2–3 minutes then turn the salmon over and cook for another 1–2 minutes for medium-rare (cook a little longer if your preference is for well done).

4. Garnish the salmon with coriander leaves. Serve with sweet and sour chilli dressing and lime halves on the side, to squeeze over. Steamed Asian greens, such as bok choy, make a good accompaniment to this dish.

* **Salmon** . . . As well as having fabulous flavour, salmon is a good source of protein and is rich in essential omega-3 fatty acids, which support healthy cholesterol levels and joint mobility. Other sources of omega-3s are flax seeds and walnuts. These superfoods have the added benefit of being high in monounsaturated fats (the good fats), which, when eaten regularly and as part of a healthy diet, can help lower unhealthy cholesterol levels.

Sweet and Sour Chilli Dressing

MAKES 1 CUP   DF | EF

⅓ cup grated palm sugar
2–3 tbsp light soy sauce
1–2 tbsp Thai fish sauce
juice of 2–3 limes
1–2 red chillies, seeds removed, finely chopped

1. Combine all ingredients in a small bowl and stir until sugar dissolves. This sauce should have a balanced taste of hot, sweet, sour and salty flavours.

2. Taste and adjust, if necessary, by adding a little more of each ingredient until the perfect balance is achieved.

3. Serve the dressing on the side or drizzled over the salmon.

Roast Pumpkin and Bulghur Salad with Walnut and Red Capsicum Dressing

Apart from the lovely caramelised flavour of this pumpkin salad, much of its value lies in its opulent orange colouring. Not only is this richness a treat to the eye, but eating a good helping of bright orange vegetables contributes hefty amounts of vitamin C, potassium, iron and fibre to our daily diets.

SERVES 6   DF | EF | V

1 cup coarse bulghur wheat
1 kg crown pumpkin, peeled and seeds removed
olive oil
2 cloves garlic, crushed
salt and freshly ground black pepper
1 tsp sweet Spanish smoked paprika
¼ cup chopped walnuts
¼ cup pumpkin seeds
Walnut and red capsicum dressing (recipe follows)
¼ cup torn fresh mint leaves

1. Preheat oven to 190 °C. Place bulghur in a bowl and cover with plenty of boiling water. Cover with a plate and set aside for 10 minutes to soften. Once soft, drain bulghur in a sieve to remove any excess water.

2. Cut pumpkin into 2-cm cubes and scatter over an oven pan. Mix 2 tablespoons of oil with crushed garlic and drizzle over pumpkin. Season with salt and pepper and sprinkle with paprika and then toss well to coat evenly.

3. Roast pumpkin for 25–30 minutes or until tender and caramelised. Remove from oven and set aside to cool.

4. Combine walnuts and pumpkin seeds in a small pan and place in oven to toast for 5–10 minutes until golden brown. Remove to cool.

5. Combine drained bulghur and roasted pumpkin in a bowl. Pour over half the dressing and toss well. Arrange the salad in a serving bowl and drizzle over the remaining dressing. Serve scattered with walnuts, pumpkin seeds and fresh mint.

✳ **Beta carotene** . . . Bright orange vegetables such as pumpkin, kumara and carrots contain high levels of beta carotene, which works to boost our defences against colds and infections, and protect our skin from sun damage. Beta carotene accumulates in the skin, so the more carotene-rich produce you eat, the more skin protection you get.

Walnut and Red Capsicum Dressing

If you are making this dressing as an accompaniment to the Roast Pumpkin and Bulghur Salad, to save time, try roasting the capsicum and walnuts in the dressing at the same time as the pumpkin.

MAKES ¾ CUP   DF | EF | GF | WF | V

1 red capsicum, cut into chunks with seeds removed
olive oil
1 clove garlic, chopped
¼ cup toasted walnuts
1 tbsp apple cider vinegar
¼ cup extra virgin olive oil
salt and freshly ground black pepper

1. Preheat oven to 190 °C. Toss capsicum in a little oil and roast in the oven for 20 minutes.
2. Place the garlic, roasted capsicum, walnuts and vinegar in the bowl of a small food processor and process to chop.
3. Add the oil and process to form a smooth paste. Season with salt and pepper to taste.

✳ **Walnuts** . . . Walnuts are rich in fibre, B vitamins, magnesium and antioxidants such as Vitamin E. They are also one of the best plant sources of protein. Nuts in general are also high in plant sterols and monounsaturated fats – the good fats that have been shown to lower unhealthy cholesterol. Walnuts, in particular, have significantly higher amounts of omega-3 fatty acids, compared to other nuts.

Marinated Tofu and Soya Bean Stir-Fry with Peanut Sauce

Made from pressed soya bean curd, tofu is plain-tasting but absorbs other flavours well and this is why I like to marinate tofu before I cook it. You can also marinate whole slabs of tofu and these are great cooked on the barbecue or grilled and then served in a bun with salad as tofu burgers.

SERVES 4   DF | EF | V

350 g firm tofu, cut into 2-cm cubes
⅓ cup light soy sauce
2 tbsp grated fresh ginger
1–2 tbsp light olive oil, for stir-frying
1 red capsicum, cut into thin strips
½ red cabbage, shredded

1 cup podded soya beans or 400-g can organic soya beans, rinsed and drained
½ cup bean or pea sprouts
3 tbsp sweet chilli sauce
extra soy sauce, if required
¼ cup chopped fresh coriander
Peanut sauce (recipe follows)

1. Place cubed tofu in a shallow bowl with soy sauce and grated ginger, toss well and leave to marinate for 1 hour.
2. Remove tofu, reserving marinade. Heat oil in a wok or large frying-pan and stir-fry the tofu in two batches, tossing regularly over high heat for 3–5 minutes until browned all over. Remove to a plate.
3. Add vegetables to pan and stir-fry over high heat for 3 minutes, tossing regularly. Return tofu to pan, along with reserved tofu marinade. Add sweet chilli sauce. Stir-fry and toss well to combine.
4. Taste for seasoning and add a little more soy sauce, if necessary. Spoon immediately into bowls and scatter with coriander. Serve with peanut sauce to spoon over.

✳ **Soy foods** . . . Soya beans and tofu are inexpensive, high-quality sources of vegetarian protein, as well as calcium, iron and B-group vitamins. Whether soy products are as good for us as we've been led to believe, there are health benefits to be gained from soy if eaten as part of a varied diet. Soy contains all seven essential amino acids, making it a complete protein. Soy products contain less saturated fat than meat and a significant amount of omega-3 fatty acids, which are good for heart health. Fermented soy products, such as tempeh, soy sauce, tamari and miso are even better for us, as these contain beneficial bacteria that help our bodies digest and draw on nutrients.

Peanut Sauce

This sauce is delicious spooned over stir-fries and salads. It also makes a brilliant dressing for noodles and, of course, is a fitting satay sauce.

MAKES 1½ CUPS   DF | EF

1 cup roasted peanuts
2 cloves garlic, peeled
1 red chilli, seeds removed, chopped
2 tbsp kecap manis
½ cup tamarind water (or substitute lemon juice)
1–2 tbsp dark soy sauce, to taste

1. Place peanuts in the bowl of a food processor and coarsely chop.
2. Add remaining ingredients and process to combine into a coarse-textured sauce, adding soy sauce to taste.

✳ **Nuts** . . . Nuts are packed with omega-3 fatty acids, which can help protect against heart disease. Peanuts and peanut butter also contain valuable vitamin E, folate (folic acid), fibre, plant protein and many minerals. Raw nuts are better than oil-roasted and salted nuts and even though nuts are full of good oils, like most things, it's best to eat them in moderation as they can be fattening.

Secret Spinach 'Paneer'

The secret is that I don't actually use paneer in this dish. Paneer is a type of fresh pressed curd cheese used in Indian cookery. I've found it's possible to cheat and use silken tofu instead, which also makes this dish dairy-free, if required. Silken tofu actually has the same texture as paneer and as tofu is bland-tasting, it is an equally perfect foil for this lightly spicy green sauce.

SERVES 4   EF | GF | WF | V

500 g spinach, washed, stems removed
2 tbsp light olive oil
1 large onion, chopped
1 tbsp finely grated fresh ginger
4 cloves garlic, chopped
1 green chilli, chopped
1 tsp cumin seeds

2 tsp ground coriander
1 tsp garam masala
⅓ cup milk (or soy milk, if preferred)
350 g silken tofu, cut into 2-cm cubes
2 tsp lemon juice
salt, to taste

1. Wilt spinach in a saucepan of boiling water for 1 minute, then drain, reserving a little of the cooking water. Plunge spinach into ice cold water to refresh and cool.

2. Drain well and place in the bowl of a food processor or blender. Blend to a smooth paste with a little cooking water and then set aside.

3. Heat oil in a large saucepan. Add onion and fry over low heat for 5–10 minutes until softened but not browned. Add ginger, garlic, chilli, cumin and coriander and cook for 1 minute to release the flavours.

4. Add spinach and a little more water, if necessary, so that the mixture is loose but not watery. Bring to the boil and simmer for 2–3 minutes. Stir in garam masala and milk.

5. Add tofu and cook for a few minutes or until spinach is creamy. Stir in lemon juice and salt to taste. Serve with basmati or brown rice, if desired.

✽ **Spinach** . . . Spinach and other dark-coloured leafy greens are super low in calories and super rich in calcium, folic acid and other vitamins, minerals and disease-fighting antioxidants. Like tomatoes, the nutritional benefits of spinach are even greater when it is cooked. However, spinach is best eaten as fresh as possible, so grow your own or buy from local farmers' markets and eat soon after purchase.

Upside-Down Tomato Tart with Olive Oil Pastry

A simple tart filling like this relies on beautifully flavoured tomatoes, so choose deep red, vine-ripened fruit. Olive oil replaces butter in this pastry and while it looks more rustic than standard pastry, it has a good texture that complements the bold, juicy, sweet tomato flavour of this upside-down tart.

SERVES 4   DF | EF | V

12 small vine-ripened tomatoes
¾ cup plain flour
½ cup wholemeal flour
¼ tsp salt
2 cloves garlic, crushed
¼ cup olive oil
¼ cup boiling hot filtered water

extra flour, for dusting
½ cup quality black olives, cut in half and pitted
olive oil, to grease pan
salt and freshly ground black pepper
1 tbsp fresh oregano leaves

1. Preheat oven to 200 °C. Cut tomatoes in half and place, cut-side down, on several layers of paper towels. Leave to drain for 10 minutes.
2. To make the pastry, place the flours and salt in a bowl and make a well in the centre. Add the garlic to the well. Pour the oil and hot water into the well. Mix together with a wooden spoon just until the mixture forms a ball of dough.
3. Turn dough out onto a work surface dusted with flour and knead briefly just until smooth. As this is a hot-water pastry it does not need to rest. Roll out pastry to a 3-mm thick, 26-cm round. Prick the base all over with a fork.
4. Lightly oil the base of a 24-cm frying-pan with an ovenproof handle and scatter with olives. Arrange tomatoes on top, cut-side down, packing them in firmly to fill the pan. Place pastry on top of tomatoes, tucking in the edges to fit neatly. The slight excess of pastry allows for shrinkage during cooking.
5. Bake for 35–40 minutes or until pastry is crisp and golden brown. Remove from oven and stand for 5 minutes, then invert the tart onto a serving board or plate. Season with salt and pepper and scatter with fresh oregano.

✱ **Tomatoes** … are a rich source of vitamins A and C and contain a powerful antioxidant called lycopene, which studies show may help reduce the risk of cancer and heart disease. To absorb the benefits of lycopene, tomatoes need to be cooked with a touch of oil, as lycopene is fat-soluble. When buying tomatoes, choose the reddest fruit you can find, as the yellow and orange varieties lack lycopene. Never store tomatoes in the fridge, as this impairs their ripening ability, taste and texture.

Berry Crumble Slice

MAKES 12 SQUARES   EF | GF | WF

125 g butter, softened
1 cup gluten-free icing sugar, sifted
1 tsp pure vanilla extract
¾ cup rice flour
1 cup tapioca flour (or cornflour)
½ cup fine desiccated coconut
2 cups fresh or frozen berries of choice
extra gluten-free icing sugar, to dust

1. Preheat oven to 180 °C. Line a 17 x 27-cm slice tin with non-stick baking paper, leaving an overhang on all sides. Place butter, icing sugar and vanilla in a bowl and beat with an electric mixer until pale and creamy.
2. Sift flours and add to the creamed mixture, along with coconut. Mix gently until a crumbly dough forms. Reserve 1 cup of dough.
3. Press remaining dough into base of prepared tin. Scatter evenly with berries and then crumble the reserved dough on top.
4. Bake for 60–70 minutes or until firm and golden brown. Cool in the tin, then cut into squares to serve dusted with icing sugar.

Mini Raspberry Financiers

MAKES 30   DF | GF | WF

4 egg whites, lightly beaten
½ cup light olive oil
finely grated zest of 1 lemon
1 tsp pure vanilla extract
1 cup gluten-free icing sugar
1 cup ground almonds (or substitute desiccated coconut)
¼ cup tapioca flour
1 cup fresh raspberries (frozen are also good)
extra gluten-free icing sugar, to dust

1. Preheat oven to 190 °C. Grease 30 mini muffin tins. Combine egg whites, oil, lemon zest, vanilla and icing sugar in a mixing bowl.
2. Add ground almonds and flour and stir until just combined. Spoon mixture into prepared tins – they should be just over half full – then top each with a raspberry.
3. Bake for 20–25 minutes or until golden brown. Allow to stand in the tins for 5 minutes before turning out onto a cooling rack to cool completely. Dust with icing sugar to serve.

Blueberry Bran Muffins

MAKES 12   DF

1 cup bran flakes
⅓ cup firmly packed brown sugar
1 tbsp honey
¾ cup apple juice
1 egg, lightly beaten
¾ cup wholemeal flour
1 tsp baking powder
1 tsp baking soda
1½ cups fresh blueberries (frozen are also good)

1. Preheat oven to 180 °C. Line a 12-hole standard muffin tin with paper cases. Place bran flakes, sugar, honey and apple juice in a bowl and set aside for 5 minutes.
2. Stir in beaten egg. Add dry ingredients and stir just enough to combine. Gently fold in blueberries.
3. Spoon mixture into paper cases and bake for 20–25 minutes or until firm and golden brown.

Low-Sugar Berry Jam

MAKES 2½ CUPS   DF | EF | GF | WF | V

600 g each blueberries, raspberries and blackberries
juice of 1 lemon
200 g raw sugar

1. Place berries, lemon juice and sugar in a large heavy-based saucepan or preserving pan. Cook over low heat, stirring until the sugar dissolves.
2. Now increase heat until mixture starts to bubble. Simmer for 10 minutes.
3. Turn up heat and boil jam, stirring frequently, for a few minutes or until setting point is reached.
4. Ladle jam into sterilised jars and seal well. Sugar is necessary for preservation and for setting jam. The amount of sugar added can be cut back, as in this recipe; however, low-sugar jam has a much shorter life and should be stored in the fridge.

✳ **Super berries** . . . Packed with antioxidants, berries are also high in potassium and vitamin C, making them a top choice for increased health benefits. Select deep-coloured berries, as the darker they are, the more antioxidants they contain.

Baked Apples

The best thing about winter must surely be the chance to enjoy sweet treats and puddings more often. The promise of a sticky dessert can warm up a cold night, and brighten the dullest of days. Meltingly soft baked apples stuffed with richly flavoured filling has got to be one of the most perfect endings to any winter meal. The gooey, almost fudgy, chocolate and nut-filled centre of these baked apples makes a lovely contrast to the softness of the flesh.

SERVES 6   EF | GF | WF | DF | V

6 cooking apples

⅓ cup almonds or walnuts, coarsely chopped

60 g quality dark chocolate (dairy-free), coarsely chopped

2 tbsp raisins, chopped

1 tbsp cocoa powder, sifted

2 tbsp liquid honey

⅓ cup maple syrup

1. Preheat oven to 180 °C. Line a baking dish with non-stick baking paper. Using an apple corer or a small, sharp knife, remove cores from apples.

2. Run a sharp knife around the middle of each apple (this allows apples to expand and not explode as they bake). Place apples in prepared baking dish.

3. Combine chopped nuts, chocolate, raisins and cocoa in a bowl. Warm honey and add to the bowl, stirring to combine with other ingredients. Pack some of this mixture into the cavity of each apple, dividing it evenly.

4. Drizzle a little maple syrup over each apple and fill the baking dish with 1 cm of cold filtered water. Bake for 40 minutes, or until apples are tender, pale golden brown and surrounded by a lovely syrupy sauce.

＊ **Apples** . . . Apples are a natural high-fibre snack – just wash and eat, as the skin contains two-thirds of the fibre and many of the antioxidants found in apples. Fibre is important for good digestive health and should be consumed in sufficient quantities everyday. Apples also provide a potent source of antioxidants, like vitamin C, that help build a strong immune system, and are rich in essential minerals, such as potassium, calcium, iron and zinc that are vital for good health. Apples have a low GI (glycemic index) meaning they release sugar into the bloodstream gradually for a longer lasting supply of energy.

Market Fresh

seasonal plates using fresh market produce

✳ **The beauty of** shopping at your local farmers' and growers' market is the abundance of fresh seasonal produce. Cooking with the seasons means that food is optimally ripe, super-fresh and not cool-stored, and so has more available nutrients for us to enjoy. Plus, fresh fruits and veggies are often less expensive when in season, meaning there's money to be saved, as well. Buying just-harvested food directly means we support independent farmers who work hard to grow excellent food crops in healthy ways. Great food doesn't have to be complicated – there's nothing more appealing than fresh seasonal produce cooked well.

Summertime Fish Cooked in Paper

In French cookery, this classical method of cooking food in a paper parcel is known as *en papillote*. The parcel holds in all the essential tastes and aromas and keeps the food wonderfully moist. Cooking food in packages is always fun, as opening the packet almost feels like unwrapping a present.

SERVES 4   DF | EF | GF | WF

4 x 180-g portions white-fleshed fish
salt and freshly ground black pepper
2 cloves garlic, thinly sliced
finely grated zest and juice of 1 lemon
1 red capsicum, seeds removed, cut into
  thin strips
1 orange capsicum, seeds removed, cut into
  thin strips

2 small courgettes, cut into thin strips
4 spring onions, cut into long, thin strips
¼ tbsp capers, rinsed and drained
1 tbsp extra virgin olive oil
4 sprigs fresh oregano
lemon wedges, to serve

1. Preheat oven to 200 °C. Cut baking paper and foil into four large circles of the same size. Place one paper circle over each circle of foil. Season fish portions with salt and pepper and place one portion in the centre of each paper circle.

2. Scatter fish with a little sliced garlic and lemon zest. Place sliced capsicums, courgettes and spring onions in a bowl and toss to combine. Arrange a quarter of the vegetables on top of each piece of fish. Scatter each with a few capers and then drizzle with a little lemon juice and oil.

3. Bring opposite sides of each circle of foil and paper together to enclose fish — fold and crimp edges together (as with pastry) to form a secure parcel. Place the parcels on an oven tray.

4. Bake for 10–15 minutes, depending on thickness of fish portions. You can tell when fish is cooked because the flesh will turn opaque and will flake easily when pressed with a fork.

5. Transfer parcels to dinner plates. Open and serve immediately, garnished with oregano and with extra lemon wedges on the side, to squeeze over.

✱ **Market fresh** . . . Be sure to buy the freshest possible fish and cook it directly to capture its goodness. When purchasing fish whole, look for fish with bright, shiny eyes (dull, opaque or sunken eyes mean the fish is not fresh). The gills should be bright red. When you poke the flesh with your finger, the flesh should bounce back, indicating that the fish is fresh. When buying filleted fish, look for plump, white fillets that smell like fresh sea-water. Do not buy fillets that smell 'fishy' or are surrounded by a puddle of cloudy liquid, as these are telltale signs that the fish is not fresh.

Summer Harvest Stew

The summer harvest of redder-than-red tomatoes, a plethora of tasty different-coloured capsicums, plump courgettes and the sweetest of sweet corn are inspiring enough to encourage a line of converts to vegetarianism. This simple stew combines the summer harvest beautifully, along with plenty of health-giving summery herbs.

SERVES 4   DF | EF | GF | WF | V

2 tbsp olive oil
I onion, chopped
2 cloves garlic, crushed
2 tbsp tomato paste
3 large, ripe tomatoes, seeds and cores removed, chopped
I litre liquid vegetable stock
2 red capsicums, seeds removed, cut into chunks
2 cobs sweet corn, kernels removed from the cob

I bunch baby fennel bulbs, trimmed and thickly sliced
3 courgettes, thickly sliced
I bunch baby carrots, trimmed and cleaned
½ cup coarsely chopped parsley
2 tbsp fresh oregano leaves
2 tbsp chopped fresh chives
juice of ½ lemon
salt and freshly ground black pepper

I. Heat a large, heavy-based saucepan, add oil and onion and cook over medium heat for 10 minutes, until onion is softened but not browned. Add garlic to pan and cook for 30 seconds more.
2. Add tomato paste and chopped tomatoes and simmer for 5 minutes. Add stock and all the vegetables. Bring mixture to the boil and then turn down heat to simmer for 10 minutes until vegetables are tender.
3. Stir in herbs and lemon juice. Check and adjust the seasoning with salt and pepper to taste.

✱ My advice . . . Herbs are full of concentrated goodness, so it's a wise and tasty choice to add fresh herbs to your cooking in liberal amounts. I adore different herbs for their aromatic qualities, pungent flavours and vivid colour.

Autumn Eggplant Red Curry

Early autumn is when a wonderful overlap occurs in the supply of end-of-summer produce with that which signifies the beginnings of winter. This is when everything edible seems to explode with intense flavour and there's often a glut of things like sun-ripened eggplants, meaning they are often both plentiful and inexpensive. Make the most of this situation by giving eggplant a starring role in this tasty curry dish.

SERVES 4   EF | GF | WF | DF | V

I large onion, coarsely chopped

4-cm piece fresh ginger, peeled and coarsely chopped

2 cloves garlic, peeled

1–2 small red chillies, seeds removed, to taste

¼ cup tomato paste

2 tsp each ground cumin, paprika and garam masala

light olive oil

500 g (I large) eggplant, cut into 1.5-cm cubes

400-g can chopped tomatoes

I cup cold filtered water

410-g can chickpeas, rinsed and drained

salt and freshly ground black pepper

¼ cup fresh coriander leaves

steamed basmati rice, to serve

1. Place onion, ginger, garlic, chillies, tomato paste and all spices into a food processor and blend to form a curry paste, or pound in a mortar with a pestle.

2. Heat 2 tablespoons of oil in a large saucepan and stir-fry the cubed eggplant in two batches, to brown on all sides, adding a little more oil, as necessary. Remove to one side.

3. Add curry paste mixture to pan and cook for 1–2 minutes, stirring continuously, to release the flavours. Stir in tomatoes, water and chickpeas and return eggplant to pan.

4. Bring mixture to the boil then turn down the heat and simmer, uncovered, for 20 minutes until sauce has thickened and eggplant is meltingly tender. Season with salt and pepper to taste. Serve scattered with coriander, with steamed basmati rice on the side.

❋ **My advice** . . . Serve traditional accompaniments with this curry, such as natural yoghurt, pappadums and mango chutney, as desired.

Mushroom Stroganoff Pie

Stroganoff is one of those popular old classics that remains a perennial favourite amongst many simply because it tastes so incredibly good. I've given the original recipe a revamp by making it meat-free and also by popping it into a pie tin and topping it with a modern gluten-free pastry crust. The crust is beautifully golden and light and works really well in contrast to the creamy and rich mushroom stroganoff filling. This is comfort food and tasty health food all in one dish.

SERVES 4   GF | WF

olive oil

2 large onions, sliced

3 cloves garlic, chopped

350 g field mushrooms, cleaned
  and thickly sliced

250 g button mushrooms,
  cleaned and quartered

¾ cup red wine

2 tbsp tomato paste

¼ cup cold filtered water

¾ cup low-fat sour cream

salt and freshly ground black
  pepper

1 batch Savoury shortcrust pastry
  (recipe follows)

1. Heat 2 tablespoons of oil in a large saucepan, add onions and cook over medium heat for 10 minutes to soften. Add garlic and cook for 1 minute more, then remove to one side.

2. Add a little more oil and pan-fry mushrooms to lightly brown. Return onions to pan. Add wine and simmer for 5 minutes, scraping any sediment from base of pan.

3. Stir in tomato paste, water and sour cream – don't let mixture boil once sour cream has been added or it may split. Season with salt and pepper to taste. Transfer mixture to a 1.5-litre capacity pie dish and set aside to cool.

4. Make pastry. Roll out pastry to 3-mm thick and just bigger than the top of the pie dish and use to cover filling. Crimp or fork edges to secure the pastry lid.

5. Roll out any scraps of pastry and use to make decorations, if desired, such as autumn leaves. Stick these onto pastry lid with a little water. Bake pie for 25–30 minutes or until pastry is golden brown.

Savoury Shortcrust Pastry

MAKES ENOUGH FOR 1 PIE CRUST   GF | WF

½ cup rice flour

¾ cup chickpea flour

⅓ cup buckwheat flour

½ tsp salt

125 g chilled butter or non-hydrogenated
  dairy-free spread, as preferred

1 egg, lightly beaten

extra chickpea flour, to dust

1. Place flours and salt in a bowl. Cube butter or dairy-free spread and add to flour. Using your fingertips, rub butter into flour until the mixture resembles fine breadcrumbs. Alternatively, this step can be done in a food processor.

2. Make a well in the centre of dry ingredients and add egg to the well. Mix together using a blunt knife.

3. Turn mixture out onto a board dusted with chickpea flour and knead lightly to bring dough together into a ball.

4. Wrap dough in greaseproof paper and chill for 30 minutes so it is easier to roll.

* **My advice** . . . Expect gluten-free pastry to have quite a different texture to pastry made with wheat flour – it will be more crumbly and may tend to crack or break as gluten generally gives structure to baked goods. However different, gluten-free pastry still has a pleasant texture and taste. The rice, chickpea and buckwheat flours used in this recipe all have great flavours in themselves, and together they give a lovely nutty edge to this pastry, which is very tasty.

Sour Orange Thai Fish Curry

Simple and quick is the only way to cook fish, resulting in flesh that is succulent and soft. Making your own curry-spice paste is a very satisfying process that results in a textural and vibrantly aromatic base to any homemade curry.

SERVES 4   DF | EF | GF | WF

2 tbsp grated palm sugar

1 red chilli, seeds removed, finely sliced

3-cm piece fresh ginger, peeled and chopped

½ tsp ground turmeric

1 small onion, chopped

2 tbsp tomato paste

4 cups liquid fish stock

700 g white-fleshed fish fillets, cut into large cubes

1 bunch gai larn, bok choy or choy sum

1 bunch spring onions, cut into 3-cm lengths

2 tbsp Thai fish sauce, to taste

juice of 3–4 limes, to taste

¼ cup coriander leaves, to garnish

extra limes, to serve

1. To make a curry-spice paste, place sugar, chilli, ginger, turmeric, onion and tomato paste in the bowl of a food processor. Process to form a thick paste, adding a little fish stock if necessary to combine.

2. Place curry paste in a large saucepan. Add fish stock and bring to the boil, stirring to combine. Add cubed fish and turn down heat to simmer gently for 5 minutes to cook fish.

3. Add gai larn and spring onions and simmer for 2 minutes more. Season with fish sauce and lime juice to taste so that the finished flavour is a balance of hot, sweet, sour and salty tastes.

4. Ladle into bowls and scatter with coriander leaves. Serve with lime halves on the side, to squeeze over.

＊ **My advice** . . . Try to buy lesser-known species of fish from your region. This practice takes the pressure off popular species of fish, meaning that fishing will be more sustainable in the future. The bonus is we get to try new tastes, as well.

Pumpkin, Pine Nut and Thyme Self-Crusting Quiche

There's something very special about the interplay of the sweet caramel flavour of pumpkin and the salty creaminess of cheese in this easy but effective self-crusting style of quiche. This quiche is very versatile — it makes a great lunchtime meal or light supper but can also double as a brunch dish or picnic fare. You can also substitute other vegetables for the pumpkin (weight for weight) to work with the seasons.

SERVES 6–8

olive oil spray

700 g (½ medium–large-sized) pumpkin, skin and seeds removed

3 spring onions, chopped

½ cup grated Edam or Cheddar, or 100 g crumbled feta

4 eggs

1 cup low-fat milk

½ cup self-raising flour or wheat- and gluten-free self-raising flour

salt and freshly ground black pepper

1 tbsp chopped fresh thyme leaves

¼ cup pine nuts

Winter pesto (optional, recipe follows)

1. Heat oven to 190 °C. Lightly spray a ceramic 1-litre-capacity quiche dish with oil. Cut pumpkin flesh into 2-cm cubes and scatter over base of dish.

2. Scatter spring onions and cheese over pumpkin. Beat eggs in a bowl, add milk and flour and whisk to combine. Season well with salt and pepper and stir in thyme.

3. Pour egg mixture over pumpkin. Bake for 15 minutes, then scatter pine nuts over surface (these are added later so they don't over-brown).

4. Continue baking for a further 20 minutes or until quiche is golden brown and set. Serve warm, cut in wedges. Serve with dollops of winter pesto, if desired.

✳ My advice . . . Cutting into a large pumpkin can be quite a dangerous exercise. Unless you have a very large knife and lots of courage, I recommend buying pumpkin already sectioned - though make sure the pumpkin pieces have been freshly cut. Being able to see inside the pumpkin is also useful so you can ensure that the flesh has a strong colour and is not pale and watery.

Winter Pesto

Lots of lemon juice gives this bright green pesto a fantastic fresh, zingy taste.

MAKES 1¼ CUPS   DF | EF | GF | WF

1 clove garlic, peeled

½ cup firmly packed spinach leaves

½ cup firmly packed parsley leaves

¼ cup firmly packed mint leaves

½ cup walnuts, cashew nuts or blanched almonds

juice of 2 lemons

¼–⅓ cup extra virgin olive oil

salt and freshly ground black pepper

1. Place garlic, spinach, parsley and mint leaves in the bowl of a food processor and pulse to chop. Add nuts and process to coarsely grind. Add lemon juice and process to combine.

2. With the motor running, add the oil through the feed tube in a thin stream until the mixture amalgamates and forms a thick paste. Season with salt and pepper to taste.

3. Place in a lidded container and cover surface with a film of oil to prevent discolouration. Store in the fridge.

Spring Green Salad with Poppy Seed Dressing

The plethora of alluring produce that comes with spring leaves us no excuse for not eating our greens. This salad is one of my favourites — it is light and crisp, fills the kitchen with fresh, spring-like aromas and is a brilliant way to incorporate a variety of greens into your daily diet. Use fresh peas and broad beans in season — the gentle process of removing the peas and beans from their pods can be kind of therapeutic, but feel free to substitute frozen ones if you can't spare the time.

SERVES 4–6   DF | EF | GF | WF | V

300 g asparagus, trimmed and cut into thirds

250 g green beans, trimmed and cut into thirds

2 small courgettes, finely sliced, or substitute baby spring fennel bulbs

200 g sugar snap peas, trimmed

1 cup podded peas

½ cup podded broad beans, skins removed

50 g baby rocket leaves, sprouts or young shoots of spring greens

Poppy seed dressing (recipe follows)

1. Cook asparagus and beans in boiling salted water for 2 minutes, then add courgettes or fennel, sugar snaps and peas and cook for 1 minute more or until just tender to the bite and still bright green.

2. Drain well and then plunge the vegetables into ice-cold water to stop the cooking process. Once cold, drain well and combine with broad beans and rocket or sprouts in a large salad bowl.

3. Pour dressing over the salad and toss well to coat.

Poppy Seed Dressing

DF | EF | GF | WF | V

1 tbsp apple cider vinegar
3 tbsp extra virgin olive oil
1 tbsp poppy seeds
salt and freshly ground black pepper

1. In a small bowl, whisk all the ingredients together to amalgamate. Season with salt and pepper to taste.

* **My advice** . . . Vinaigrette proportions can be varied. Add more acidity (vinegar, verjuice, citrus juice) or oil according to personal taste, or according to the tartness of the food being dressed. If left to stand, oil and lemon juice or vinegar will separate, so whisk dressing together again just before serving.

Barbecued Spring Asparagus with Parmesan Dressing

Asparagus takes on a slightly nutty flavour when barbecued. Serve this salad warm so that the Parmesan in the dressing melts and mingles with the flavour of the asparagus.

SERVES 4   DF | GF | WF

2 x 300-g bunches fresh
  asparagus, woody ends
  snapped off
2 cloves garlic, crushed
1 tbsp balsamic vinegar

3 tbsp olive oil
salt and freshly ground black
  pepper
Parmesan dressing (recipe
  follows)

1. Preheat a chargrill pan or barbecue to a high heat. Place asparagus spears in a bowl with garlic, balsamic and oil. Season with salt and pepper and toss well to coat.
2. Chargrill or barbecue asparagus for 2 minutes each side, turning once during cooking.
3. Serve asparagus with Parmesan dressing on the side to spoon over.

✳ **Asparagus** . . . Asparagus is one of the most nutritionally well-balanced vegetables in existence. It contains no cholesterol, close to no fat or carbohydrates and is high in iron, protein, fibre, vitamins and potassium. To be sure to gain the maximum health benefits of asparagus, always cook it soon after purchase. Some recipes demand that asparagus spears be peeled, but only peel those that are particularly thick and woody, as valuable nutrients are lost with the discarded peel. The best way to prepare asparagus is to wash the spears and snap off the tough end portions, retaining as much of the tender green spears as possible.

Parmesan Dressing

MAKES ¾ CUP   EF | GF | WF

1 tsp Dijon mustard
1 clove garlic, crushed
2 tsp lemon juice
salt and freshly ground black pepper
⅓ cup low-fat sour cream
2 tbsp cold water
¼ cup finely grated Parmesan

1. In a small bowl, whisk all dressing ingredients together until smooth.
2. Stored in the fridge, this dressing lasts well for up to 4 days.

Shop Smart, Recycle, Reuse

We are all beginning to notice the damage we have done and are doing to our world. By changing some of our habits, we can do a significant amount to make the world a better place. Here are some easily achievable ideas to start you on your way to improving your own little world and, in turn, the whole world. For those who have already started to live a better life, here's some more inspiration to keep you going in the right direction.

We can lesson our impact on the environment by shopping smart, recycling and reusing household items as much as possible. I find this sort of efficiency provides a huge sense of satisfaction and actually relieves stress, as well. The other great benefit is that, by following these ideas, we can all save money and the environment.

Shop Smart

By creating a demand as consumers, we encourage the supply of honest, natural products from ecologically sound, sustainable sources. A good way to do this is to support independent shopkeepers and farmers who bring us these products. Choose to buy natural and organic foods (see page 116) and use eco-friendly household cleaning ingredients (see page 200), whenever possible. Use a basket for small shopping trips and shop on foot, if and when you can.

I look forward to my weekly forage at my local farmers' and growers' market. The beauty of these markets, which are thankfully springing up everywhere, is the seasonal freshness of the organic produce. There is often also unique produce to buy that you'd never find in a supermarket, like fabulous heirloom tomatoes or organic miniature pears. I love the massive bundles of herbs that I use to supplement my own homegrown supply — when I need to make a particularly big batch of pesto, for example.

Say No to Plastics

We can choose to avoid excessively packaged products, as disposal of all this waste has a direct and very negative impact on the environment. Start by choosing produce that is loose rather than packed in polystyrene trays and wrapped in plastic. At my local greengrocer, I now ask for my vegetables to be packed in a cardboard box instead of plastic bags. Most of us are now in the habit of taking a basket or reusable cloth shopping bag with us instead of relying on plastic carrier bags, and this is a really good step towards lessening our reliance on plastic.

Another sound move we can make is to reduce the use of plastic wrap in the kitchen. Plastic wrap is a relatively modern invention that our mothers and grandmothers managed perfectly well without. I've gone back to covering bowls of food with a plate — this makes stacking bowls in the fridge really easy, too. I also use bowls to cover food heated in the microwave, as when overheated, plastic wrap can impart toxins into the food. Pack portable food directly into reusable lunchboxes or wrap in greaseproof paper. I happily save paper bags, brown paper, wrapping papers, useful small cardboard boxes (like shoe boxes) and even envelopes and pieces of string for other purposes in the kitchen and around the house.

Recycle

Make the most of your local council recycling collections to recycle paper, cans, glass and plastic containers. Better still, find uses for some of these vessels around the house. Bottles and jars are perfect for homemade sauces and jams. Small lidded jars work well for storing aromatic spices, too. Pretty bottles make nice vases for a posy of garden flowers. And plastic containers can be used for propagating plants or as mini hothouses for baby plants.

Start collecting raw fruit and vegetable peelings and other food scraps and create compost for the garden (see Start a Kitchen Garden page 50). Composting not only provides valuable nutrients to enrich garden soil and plants but lessens landfill waste and high carbon emissions from its slow decomposition. Composting, therefore, is a very real way we can give back to Mother Nature.

Reuse, Collect and Enjoy

One of my favourite ways to recycle and reuse is to buy vintage kitchen equipment, cutlery, crockery and glassware. The ritual of discovery around finding such lasting treasures provides me with a lot of personal pleasure; it's also good economy, eco-friendly and now very chic.

It's easy and fun to get into the habit of visiting local vintage shops, charity op-shops, flea markets and garage sales to hunt for and gather beautiful pieces of old china. Don't worry if it's all different, as eclectic, mismatched pieces are much more interesting than boring duplicates. I've got wonderful collections of delicate tea cups and saucers and pretty plates, remarkable old serving platters, interesting looking cutlery, and sturdy carving implements, all of which I regularly put to good use.

Modern, mass production means items like these are just not made the same anymore. It's also possible to pick up highly appealing, unique pieces for a fraction of the cost of a new version. Reusing rustic pieces and beautiful old things gives them a new, extended life and is a brilliant way of recycling. Plus, it feels good to show

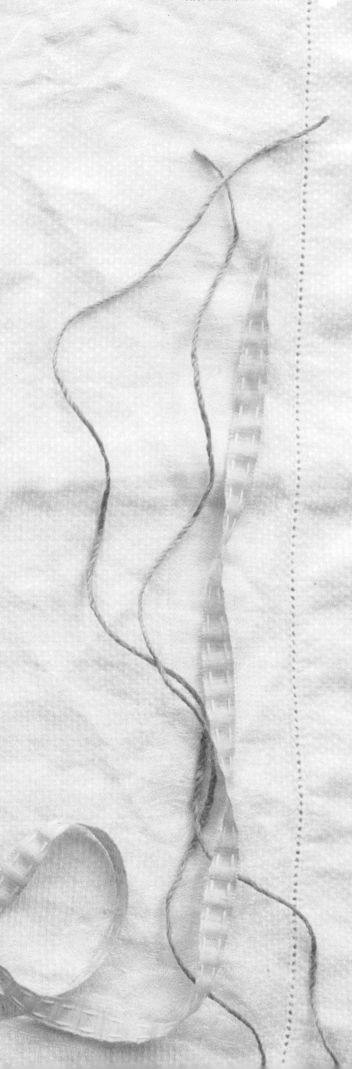

appreciation for the timeless qualities, classic charm and worthy craftsmanship of bygone eras.

You'll find old kitchen linen is also very collectable and useful. Pre-loved vintage tea towels, tablecloths and napkins can be washed as good as new and they retain their sturdiness and character, too. Squirt some fresh lemon juice on any stains to naturally bleach and remove them. Admire delicate made-by-hand details and take great pleasure in using these items, as they were made for this purpose and not to be stored away in a cupboard.

"Find uses for vessels around the house. Bottles and jars are perfect for homemade sauces and jams. Small lidded jars work well for storing aromatic spices, too."

I find vintage jugs particularly attractive and useful for drinks, sauces and dressings. I also find some water jugs can work perfectly to hold a pretty bunch of flowers. I seek out attractive old glass jars, as these are perfect for filling with homemade preserves, jams and relishes, which can make great gifts from the kitchen. Lidded jars also make excellent, hygienic storage containers for kitchen pantry staples, like flours, grains and pulses. Small jars are excellent for shaking up vinaigrettes for salads, and small bottles are perfect receptacles to hold a single lovely bloom.

Ever since I was a teenager I've collected old kitchen utensils, like egg beaters, which are often more efficient than many modern versions. I find old utensils aesthetically pleasing, plus I feel an emotional connection with items that have been pre-loved and have a story to tell of the cooks who may have used them. This form of reuse ties in beautifully with our sense of nostalgia for our childhood experiences, such as the baking our grandmothers made for us. I'm sure this is part of the reason why we're now returning to pursuits like home baking — simply because it makes us feel good.

Go with the Grain

wonder grains, seeds and dried legumes

* **Grains and dried legumes** are powerful foods. Incredibly satisfying in their own right, legumes and some ancient grains provide an excellent and inexpensive source of natural plant-based protein. Grains act as flavour sponges, soaking up the nuances of any stocks, herbs and spices that surround them. Dried pulses, such as peas, beans and lentils, are a versatile, delicious and long-respected food source. These healthy, cheap and cheerful staples have enormous culinary potential and can be used to create vegetarian delights and side dishes for other forms of protein.

Creamy Polenta

If you've ever had polenta and not enjoyed it, please try my recipe and give polenta one more chance. Not only is it delicious in taste and texture, but this method makes polenta production stress free and leaves you with a clean saucepan, which other versions don't!

SERVES 6   EF | GF | WF

4 cups cold filtered water

2 tbsp olive oil

4 cloves garlic, peeled and crushed

1 cup polenta

50 g butter

½ cup freshly grated Parmesan

salt and freshly ground black pepper

Caramelised onion, tomato and black olive sauce (recipe follows), optional

2 tbsp oregano leaves

1. In a heavy-based saucepan, bring water to the boil, add oil and garlic and then rain in polenta, stirring constantly to combine. Simmer for 10 minutes.

2. Add butter to melt and then cover saucepan, turn off heat and allow polenta to steam and soften for 30 minutes. Place the pan over a medium heat for 5 minutes, stirring to reheat the polenta.

3. Stir in Parmesan. Season generously with salt and pepper and stir well. Serve the polenta as a savoury porridge topped with caramelised onion, tomato and black olive sauce (recipe follows) and sprinkle with oregano leaves if desired.

4. Alternatively, turn the polenta out into a dish moistened with water, allow to set then cut into pieces and grill or fry until crisp and hot. This recipe makes a large amount, so any leftover polenta can also be prepared in this way at a later date. Serve as an accompaniment to meat or vegetable dishes.

✳ Polenta . . . Polenta refers to both the uncooked corn meal (ground dried corn) and also the cooked savoury porridge-like dish. Polenta is traditionally a staple dish of northern Italy but is now enjoyed by people all over the world who love Italian cuisine.

Caramelised Onion, Tomato and Black Olive Sauce

An extremely tasty sauce like this one makes a perfect topping to creamy polenta.

SERVES 6   DF | EF | GF | WF | V

2 tbsp olive oil

2 onions, finely sliced

2 tsp brown sugar

1 tbsp balsamic vinegar

½ cup red wine

400-g can chopped tomatoes

½ cup pitted black olives, coarsely chopped

salt and freshly ground black pepper

1. Heat oil in a saucepan, then add onions and cook over medium heat for 10 minutes, stirring often, until softened but not browned.

2. Add sugar and balsamic vinegar; turn up the heat a little and cook for 5 minutes more to lightly caramelise. Add wine and simmer for 5 minutes to reduce.

3. Add canned tomatoes and any juice and simmer for 10 minutes until the liquid is reduced and the sauce thick.

4. Stir in olives and season with salt and pepper to taste. Serve with creamy polenta.

Chilli Black Bean Pies Topped with Vegetable Mash

SERVES 4   EF | GF | WF

VEGETABLE MASH
400 g floury potatoes (such as Agria), peeled and cut into chunks
400 g kumara, peeled and cut into chunks
400 g carrots, peeled and cut into chunks
¼ cup extra virgin olive oil
½ cup warmed milk of your choice
salt and freshly ground black pepper

1. Cook the potatoes, kumara and carrots in boiling salted water for 10–15 minutes or until very tender. Drain well and mash. While still hot, add olive oil and milk and beat until smooth and fluffy. Season with salt and pepper to taste.

CHILLI BLACK BEAN FILLING
2 tbsp olive oil
1 onion, diced
3 cloves garlic, chopped
1 red chilli, seeds removed, finely chopped
2 stalks celery, finely diced
420-g can black beans, rinsed and drained
2 tbsp tomato paste
400-g can chopped tomatoes
1½ cups sweet corn kernels (taken from 1 cob of corn)
3 tbsp chopped fresh parsley or coriander
salt and freshly ground black pepper

1. To make the filling, heat a saucepan, add oil, onion, garlic, chilli and celery and cook over medium–low heat for 10 minutes, stirring regularly, until vegetables are softened but not browned.
2. Add black beans, tomato paste, canned tomatoes and any juice and simmer for 10 minutes until the liquid is reduced and the sauce is thick. Stir in the corn kernels and parsley or coriander and season with salt and pepper to taste.
3. Preheat oven to 180 °C. Divide the bean mixture between four 1½-cup-capacity ovenproof dishes or ramekins. Top each with a portion of vegetable mash. Bake for 20–25 minutes or until the topping is golden brown.

* **Natural selection** . . . Like most legumes, black beans are cholesterol-free, virtually fat-free, and high in fibre and nutrients, supplying more than half the daily requirement of folic acid and sizable amounts of calcium, magnesium, iron and zinc in every serving. Dried beans are also loaded with phytochemicals, known to lower the risk of heart disease and some cancers.

Quinoa Paella

Quinoa (pronounced keen-wah) is usually referred to, and cooked, as a grain, but is actually the seed of a herbal plant. High in complete protein and gluten-free, these tiny ivory-coloured beads have a wonderful nutty taste. Widely available from health-food stores and some supermarkets, this nutritional wonder grain cooks quickly to give texture and crunch to salads, soups and baked dishes and can be used in place of rice or pasta in many recipes. While not remotely traditional to Spanish Paella, I find quinoa works well in this magnificent stand-alone main dish.

SERVES 6   DF | EF | GF | WF

½ tsp saffron threads
¼ cup filtered boiling water
1½ cups quinoa
olive oil
500 g chicken breast or thigh meat, cut in
  2-cm cubes
1 red onion, diced
3 cloves garlic, crushed
2 tsp sweet Spanish smoked paprika

½ cup tomato purée
3 tomatoes, coarsley diced
1½ cups liquid chicken stock
3 tbsp chopped fresh parsley
salt and freshly ground black pepper
12 peeled prawns, deveined
12 mussels, scrubbed
1 red capsicum, thinly sliced with seeds
  removed

1. Combine saffron with boiling water in a small bowl and set aside for 10 minutes to dissolve. Rinse quinoa thoroughly in cold running water to remove the natural bitter coating and drain well.

2. Heat a paella (traditional paella pan) or substitute a large frying-pan, add a little oil and cook the cubed chicken for 5 minutes to brown all over. Remove to one side.

3. Add onion and a little more oil to the pan and cook for 5 minutes until the onion has softened. Add garlic and paprika and cook for 30 seconds more. Add tomato purée, tomatoes, dissolved saffron and stock and bring to the boil.

4. Stir in quinoa, chicken and parsley and season with salt and pepper. Arrange prawns, mussels and sliced red capsicum on the surface of the dish. Cook over a medium heat for 20 minutes, without stirring, until liquid has evaporated, the mussels have opened and quinoa is tender to the bite.

✽   **Paella** . . . Paella is the name of the specialised pan the food is cooked in and also the name of the finished rice dish. A frying-pan can be used if you don't have a special paella pan. Do not stir the paella as it cooks, this way a golden brown crust of rice forms in the base of the pan and is a much prized part of the dish.

Red Kidney Bean Curry with Amaranth Pilaf

Red Kidney Bean Curry

Traditionally called Ramja, I fell in love with the wonderful flavours of this curry on my last trip to India. I have to admit that I'd never thought of using kidney beans in an Indian curry, so this was a delicious revelation. This is the sort of dish that tastes even better the next day, so make plenty so you can enjoy the leftovers.

SERVES 6   EF | GF | WF | DF | V

- -

2 tbsp light olive oil
2 onions, finely chopped
3-cm piece ginger, finely chopped
6 cloves garlic, crushed
2 fresh green chillies, finely chopped with seeds removed
2 tsp ground coriander seeds
1 tsp cumin seeds
1 tsp garam masala
2 large tomatoes, coarsely chopped
2 x 400-g cans red kidney beans, rinsed and drained
4 cups cold filtered water
salt, to taste

- -

1. Heat oil in a large heavy-based saucepan. Add onions and cook over medium heat for 10 minutes until softened but not browned.
2. Add ginger, garlic, chillies, coriander seeds, cumin seeds and garam masala and fry for 1 minute to release flavours.
3. Add tomatoes, red kidney beans and water and cook for 10–15 minutes or until the beans are very soft.
4. Roughly mash some of the beans to thicken the sauce and season with salt to taste.

* **Beans** . . . Beans may be small in size, but they're big in fibre and iron. Darker coloured beans, such as kidney beans, have the highest concentration of all beans.

Amaranth Pilaf

Amaranth makes a great base for pilaf in place of the usual rice. It is an important ingredient in Indian cuisine where it is known as rajeera — the king's grain.

SERVES 4   DF | EF | GF | WF | V

- -

2 tbsp olive oil
1 onion, finely diced
1 tbsp ground coriander
1 tsp each ground cumin and turmeric
¼ tsp chilli powder
2 cups liquid vegetable stock
1¼ cups amaranth
⅓ cup dried currants
⅓ cup toasted slivered almonds
⅓ cup chopped fresh coriander
salt and freshly ground black pepper

- -

1. Preheat oven to 180 °C. Heat oil in an ovenproof casserole dish, add onion and cook for 10 minutes to soften but not brown. Add spices and fry for 1 minute to release flavours.
2. Add stock and bring mixture to the boil. Stir in amaranth. Cover casserole dish and bake for 20 minutes, or until amaranth is translucent and liquid has been absorbed.
3. Stir in currants, almonds and coriander and season with salt and pepper to taste. Serve with red kidney bean curry, if desired.

* **Amaranth** . . . An ancient South American staple and naturally gluten-free, amaranth gives a high nutritional bang for your buck. Amaranth is one of the best plant-based sources of complete protein, iron and magnesium and has three times the calcium of milk. Technically not a grain but, rather, the seed of a plant, amaranth has a distinctive sweet, peppery taste and so is often combined with rice, for a more mellow flavour.

Millet, Watercress and Marinated Asparagus Salad

Infinitely useful, this salad can be served anytime — either as a starter to charm your guests' taste-buds while you get other dishes ready, as a side dish, or as a main course for a summer picnic, casual lunch or simple evening meal.

SERVES 4–6   EF | GF | WF

½ cup millet
300-g bunch fine asparagus
  spears
Watercress dressing
  (recipe follows)

150 g feta, crumbled (optional)
1 cup watercress leaves, picked
  from the stems

Watercress Dressing

MAKES ½ CUP   DF | EF | GF | WF | V

3 cloves garlic, peeled
1 cup watercress, tightly packed
¼ cup extra virgin olive oil
salt and freshly ground black pepper

1. Place garlic and watercress in the bowl of a food processor and pulse to chop.
2. With the motor running, pour in oil slowly to form a smooth dressing. Season with salt and pepper to taste.

1. Cook millet in plenty of boiling water for 12–15 minutes or until tender to the bite. Drain, rinse in cold water and drain well.
2. Finely slice asparagus on an angle, discarding the woody ends, and place in a large salad bowl. Make watercress dressing and pour over asparagus. Leave to marinate for 30 minutes.
3. Add cold millet to marinated asparagus and dressing and toss well to combine. Mix in crumbled feta and watercress leaves.

✳ **Millet** . . . Another gluten-free plant seed, millet is not just for the birds. I use it in place of rice or pasta in many dishes. With a lovely, mildly sweet, toasted-corn flavour, millet is an interesting, tasty, nutritious, heart-friendly alternative to other grains. This easily digested food is a rich source of protein and iron and also provides important magnesium, potassium, calcium and B vitamins.

✳ **Clever idea** . . . Many people don't realise that asparagus can also be eaten raw. Delicious and nutritious, it's best to choose tender, thin spears for this purpose. Dice, slice or shave raw asparagus and add to salads, or marinate in olive oil to create a crunchy vegetable treat.

Buckwheat, Eggplant and Tomato Salad

Buckwheat makes a great base for a summer salad. Its slightly nutty flavour is complemented in this salad by the addition of lots of vibrant summer herbs and the delightful kick of garlic, lemon and salty feta cheese.

SERVES 4   EF | GF | WF

1 large eggplant, cut into large cubes	2 cloves garlic, crushed
olive oil	¼ cup chopped fresh basil
salt and freshly ground black pepper	¼ cup chopped fresh parsley
8 small vine-ripened tomatoes	juice of 2 lemons
1 cup wholegrain buckwheat	100 g feta or goat's cheese, crumbled

1. Preheat oven to 200 °C. Place cubed eggplant in a roasting pan. Drizzle well with oil and season with salt and pepper. Roast for 20 minutes, tossing once during cooking, until golden brown. Remove to cool.
2. Place tomatoes in a separate oven pan, drizzle with oil and season with salt and pepper. Roast for 10–15 minutes until golden brown. Remove to cool.
3. At the same time, cook buckwheat in boiling water for 6 minutes, or until tender to the bite. Drain well and set aside to cool.
4. Place eggplant, buckwheat, garlic, basil and parsley in a salad bowl. Drizzle with lemon juice, season with salt and pepper and toss well. Serve topped with baked tomatoes and crumbled feta or goat's cheese.

* **Buckwheat** . . . Commonly thought to be a grain, buckwheat is actually a fruit seed, related to rhubarb and sorrel. Naturally gluten-free, buckwheat flour is suitable for people who are sensitive to other grains that contain gluten. Energising and highly nutritious, whole buckwheat, sometimes known as groats, can be served as an alternative to rice or pasta. High in fibre, protein, essential amino acids and nutrients, buckwheat can help lower blood-glucose levels and is therefore particularly beneficial to diabetics.

Butter Bean Soup

SERVES 4   DF | EF | GF | WF | V

1 tbsp olive oil
1 onion, finely chopped
3 cloves garlic, chopped
2 x 400-g cans butter beans, rinsed and drained
3 cups liquid vegetable stock
1 tbsp chopped fresh sage or rosemary
salt and freshly ground black pepper
extra virgin olive oil, to garnish
¼ cup chopped fresh parsley
½ tsp chilli powder

1. Heat oil in a large, heavy-based saucepan. Add onion and cook for 10 minutes until softened but not browned. Add garlic and cook for 1 minute more.
2. Stir in beans and stock and bring mixture to the boil. Turn down the heat and simmer for 5 minutes. Add sage or rosemary.
3. Purée mixture in a blender and return to the pan. Simmer for 5 minutes more and then season with salt and pepper to taste.
4. Serve piping hot in bowls, drizzled with oil and scattered with parsley and a little chilli powder to taste. Serve with wholegrain or gluten-free bread on the side, as desired.

Summer Herb and Brown Rice Salad

SERVES 4   DF | EF | GF | WF | V

1¼ cups short-grain brown rice
¼ cup chopped fresh mint
¼ cup chopped fresh basil
¼ cup chopped fresh parsley
¼ cup chopped fresh coriander
1 small head radicchio, finely shredded crossways
1 red chilli, seeds removed, finely chopped
½ cup pistachio nuts, toasted, coarsely chopped
1 clove garlic, crushed
juice of 1 lemon
3 tbsp extra virgin olive oil
salt and freshly ground black pepper

1. Cook rice in plenty of boiling water for 30 minutes, or until just tender to the bite.
2. Drain well and rinse with cold water to cool. Drain well and place in a salad bowl.
3. Add remaining ingredients, season with salt and pepper and toss well.

Lemony Bulghur with Toasted Seeds

SERVES 4   DF | EF | V

1 cup bulghur wheat
2 cups liquid vegetable or chicken stock or cold filtered water
finely grated zest and juice of 1 lemon
¼ cup toasted sesame seeds
½ cup toasted sunflower seeds
½ cup toasted pumpkin seeds
½ cup chopped fresh coriander leaves
3 tbsp extra virgin olive oil
salt and freshly ground black pepper
1 red capsicum, very finely sliced

1. Place bulghur in a bowl. Heat stock or water with the lemon zest and juice until boiling and then pour this over the bulghur.
2. Stir briefly, then cover the bowl with a plate and leave bulghur to steam and soften for 10 minutes.
3. Remove covering and drain off any excess liquid. Add toasted seeds and coriander. Drizzle with oil, season with salt and pepper and toss well to combine. Top with sliced red capsicum.

Chilli Chickpea and Tomato Stew

SERVES 6   DF | EF | GF | WF | V

2 tbsp olive oil
3 medium red onions, cut into wedges
3 cloves garlic, chopped
1 red chilli, seeds removed, chopped
2 x 400-g cans chickpeas, rinsed and drained
2 x 400-g cans chopped tomatoes
salt and freshly ground black pepper
⅓ cup chopped fresh coriander

1. Heat oil in a saucepan, add onion wedges and cook over medium–high heat for 10 minutes, tossing regularly, until softened and lightly browned.
2. Add garlic and chilli and cook for 30 seconds more. Add chickpeas and tomatoes and simmer for 5–10 minutes until liquid has reduced and sauce is thick.
3. Season with salt and pepper to taste. Serve scattered with fresh coriander.

✳   Natural selection . . . With a low glycemic index (GI), high-fibre foods, like whole grains and pulses, help regulate blood-sugar levels, as well as appetite. Using a magic combination of water and fibre, these foods fill us up on fewer calories and sustain us for longer.

Buckwheat Flour Galettes

A galette is a delicious savoury French crêpe made with buckwheat flour. Gallettes can be filled with a variety of fillings from classic cheese and ham or tomato to more elaborate concoctions. Traditionally made, buckwheat crêpes are wonderfully lacy and crisp and make a great brunch or lunch dish.

MAKES 8 GF | WF

I cup buckwheat flour
¼ tsp salt
2 eggs
½ cup milk
½ cup cold filtered water
olive oil, for frying
salt and freshly ground black pepper

SUGGESTED TOPPINGS
I cup grated Gruyère or 100 g crumbled feta
4 tomatoes, sliced
a few fresh chives or torn fresh basil leaves, as preferred

1. Combine flour and salt in a bowl and make a well in the centre. In another bowl, beat the eggs with the milk and water. Slowly add the liquid into the well while whisking continuously to incorporate flour and form a smooth batter. Cover with a plate and set aside to rest for 30 minutes.
2. Before cooking the crêpes, whisk a little more water into the batter to bring it to a pouring consistency. Heat a non-stick pan over medium–high heat. Add a film of oil to the pan. Add a quarter of a cupful of batter to the pan, immediately tilting the pan from side to side to swirl the mixture and evenly coat the base of the pan with batter.
3. Cook for I minute or until crisp and golden then flip over and cook the other side for 30 seconds. Repeat with remaining mixture until you have used all the batter, stacking the crêpes on a plate as they are made.
4. Fill finished crêpes with some grated Gruyère or feta and sliced tomato, season with salt and pepper and fold in the sides of the crêpes to enclose the filling.
5. To serve, either heat the filled crêpes in a frying-pan or place in an oven preheated to 180 °C for 5 minutes. Scatter with chives or torn basil and serve immediately.

✳ **Buckwheat flour** . . . Buckwheat flour has a distinctive flavour and is a tasty and healthy gluten-free alternative to standard flour. Traditionally used in French galettes (savoury crêpes), it gives them a lovely nutty flavour and special crispness. Look for buckwheat flour in health-food stores if you can't find it in your local supermarket.

Lemony Bulghur with Toasted Seeds

SERVES 4   DF | EF | V

1 cup bulghur wheat
2 cups liquid vegetable or chicken stock or cold filtered water
finely grated zest and juice of 1 lemon
¼ cup toasted sesame seeds
½ cup toasted sunflower seeds
½ cup toasted pumpkin seeds
½ cup chopped fresh coriander leaves
3 tbsp extra virgin olive oil
salt and freshly ground black pepper
1 red capsicum, very finely sliced

1. Place bulghur in a bowl. Heat stock or water with the lemon zest and juice until boiling and then pour this over the bulghur.
2. Stir briefly, then cover the bowl with a plate and leave bulghur to steam and soften for 10 minutes.
3. Remove covering and drain off any excess liquid. Add toasted seeds and coriander. Drizzle with oil, season with salt and pepper and toss well to combine. Top with sliced red capsicum.

Chilli Chickpea and Tomato Stew

SERVES 6   DF | EF | GF | WF | V

2 tbsp olive oil
3 medium red onions, cut into wedges
3 cloves garlic, chopped
1 red chilli, seeds removed, chopped
2 x 400-g cans chickpeas, rinsed and drained
2 x 400-g cans chopped tomatoes
salt and freshly ground black pepper
⅓ cup chopped fresh coriander

1. Heat oil in a saucepan, add onion wedges and cook over medium–high heat for 10 minutes, tossing regularly, until softened and lightly browned.
2. Add garlic and chilli and cook for 30 seconds more. Add chickpeas and tomatoes and simmer for 5–10 minutes until liquid has reduced and sauce is thick.
3. Season with salt and pepper to taste. Serve scattered with fresh coriander.

✳ **Natural selection** . . . With a low glycemic index (GI), high-fibre foods, like whole grains and pulses, help regulate blood-sugar levels, as well as appetite. Using a magic combination of water and fibre, these foods fill us up on fewer calories and sustain us for longer.

Buckwheat Flour Galettes

A galette is a delicious savoury French crêpe made with buckwheat flour. Gallettes can be filled with a variety of fillings from classic cheese and ham or tomato to more elaborate concoctions. Traditionally made, buckwheat crêpes are wonderfully lacy and crisp and make a great brunch or lunch dish.

MAKES 8   GF | WF

1 cup buckwheat flour
¼ tsp salt
2 eggs
½ cup milk
½ cup cold filtered water
olive oil, for frying
salt and freshly ground black pepper

SUGGESTED TOPPINGS
1 cup grated Gruyère or 100 g crumbled feta
4 tomatoes, sliced
a few fresh chives or torn fresh basil leaves,
  as preferred

1. Combine flour and salt in a bowl and make a well in the centre. In another bowl, beat the eggs with the milk and water. Slowly add the liquid into the well while whisking continuously to incorporate flour and form a smooth batter. Cover with a plate and set aside to rest for 30 minutes.

2. Before cooking the crêpes, whisk a little more water into the batter to bring it to a pouring consistency. Heat a non-stick pan over medium–high heat. Add a film of oil to the pan. Add a quarter of a cupful of batter to the pan, immediately tilting the pan from side to side to swirl the mixture and evenly coat the base of the pan with batter.

3. Cook for 1 minute or until crisp and golden then flip over and cook the other side for 30 seconds. Repeat with remaining mixture until you have used all the batter, stacking the crêpes on a plate as they are made.

4. Fill finished crêpes with some grated Gruyère or feta and sliced tomato, season with salt and pepper and fold in the sides of the crêpes to enclose the filling.

5. To serve, either heat the filled crêpes in a frying-pan or place in an oven preheated to 180 °C for 5 minutes. Scatter with chives or torn basil and serve immediately.

✳ **Buckwheat flour** . . . Buckwheat flour has a distinctive flavour and is a tasty and healthy gluten-free alternative to standard flour. Traditionally used in French galettes (savoury crêpes), it gives them a lovely nutty flavour and special crispness. Look for buckwheat flour in health-food stores if you can't find it in your local supermarket.

Lentil Burgers with Red Capsicum Relish

These burgers are not your average vegetarian meal, in fact they are better! The mouth-watering, moist patties can be combined with any of your favourite burger ingredients.

SERVES 6 DF | EF | V

1 cup green or brown lentils, well washed
1 bay leaf
2 tbsp olive oil
1 onion, diced
2 cloves garlic, crushed
1 cup toasted walnuts
2 tbsp each chopped parsley and oregano
salt and freshly ground black pepper

olive oil, for pan-frying
6 sourdough or wholegrain burger buns, cut in half and toasted
3 tomatoes, sliced
100 g rocket leaves
1 avocado, sliced
Red capsicum relish (recipe follows)

1. Place lentils and bay leaf in a saucepan and cover with cold filtered water. Bring to the boil, then turn down heat and simmer for 20 minutes or until tender. Drain and set aside to cool.

2. At the same time, heat oil in a pan, add onion and cook over medium heat for 10 minutes until softened but not browned. Add garlic and cook for 1 minute more. Remove to cool.

3. Place cold lentils and onion mixture in the bowl of a food processor with walnuts and herbs. Process to form a rough-textured paste and season with salt and pepper. Mould the mixture into six even-sized patties.

4. Pan-fry patties in a little oil over medium heat until golden brown on each side – this takes 3–4 minutes on each side. Place one lentil pattie on the base of each burger bun. Top with salad ingredients and serve immediately, with red capsicum relish on the side.

✳ Natural selection . . . Tiny but nutritionally mighty, lentils contain important minerals, B-vitamins and protein. Lentils are also an excellent source of cholesterol-lowering fibre, which helps prevent blood-sugar levels from rising rapidly after a meal. Lentils do not require soaking before cooking but should be washed well first. Do not add salt to the cooking water, as this can make the lentils tough. Simply season lentils after cooking.

Red Capsicum Relish

Fresh relish will last well for up to a week, if stored in the fridge. Bring to room temperature to serve.

MAKES 2½ CUPS DF | EF | GF | WF | V

2 red capsicums, seeds removed, finely diced
1 small red onion, finely diced
⅓ cup pitted black olives, chopped
2 tbsp chopped fresh parsley
2 tbsp balsamic vinegar
½ cup extra virgin olive oil
salt and freshly ground black pepper

1. Place all ingredients in a bowl, season with salt and pepper and stir well to combine.
2. Cover bowl with a plate and leave to marinate for at least 2 hours, or preferably overnight, in the fridge.
3. To serve, bring to room temperature and drain off the oil. The flavoured oil can be reserved and used in salad dressings or for cooking.

Barley and Pumpkin Risotto

Risotto is one of those wonderfully flavoursome dishes that leaves you wondering what you ate before you discovered it. This version is made with barley instead of rice. Barley takes a lot longer to cook but doesn't need constant stirring, so you can do other things at the same time. When cooked in this method, barley develops a rich creamy texture and a gorgeous nutty flavour and makes a very satisfying meal.

SERVES 4   EF | WF

5 cups liquid vegetable stock

2 tbsp tomato paste

olive oil

1 large onion, finely diced

2 cloves garlic, crushed

1½ cups hulled or pearl barley

½ cup white wine

2 cups (300 g) coarsely grated pumpkin
  (or substitute kumara, if preferred)

2 tbsp butter or extra virgin olive oil

salt and freshly ground black pepper

2 tbsp fresh sage leaves

1. Heat stock and tomato paste in a small saucepan. Heat 2 tablespoons of oil in a large, heavy-based saucepan, add onion and cook over medium heat for 10 minutes until softened but not browned.

2. Add the garlic and barley to pan and cook for 2 minutes, stirring continuously. Add wine and bring mixture to the boil, stirring until wine is well reduced.

3. Add half a cup of hot stock and simmer gently, stirring until liquid is reduced. Continue in this way, adding stock half a cupful at a time and simmering the mixture, stirring occasionally, until the barley is tender (this should take about 40 minutes).

4. Add grated pumpkin with the final cupful of stock and cook until the pumpkin is tender. Stir in butter or oil to add a little extra richness to the risotto and season with salt and pepper to taste. Turn off the heat, cover the pan and allow the mixture to steam for 5 minutes to finish cooking. This will make the texture of the barley light and fluffy.

5. Heat a little oil in a small frying-pan over a high heat and cook the sage leaves for 30 seconds until crisp. Drain on paper towels. To serve the risotto, stir in a little extra stock, if necessary, to give the sauce a sloppy consistency. Serve in bowls topped with fried sage leaves.

*   Barley . . . Barley has a nutty flavour and appealing chewy texture and is one of the most nutritious cereal grains. In addition to providing selenium, phosphorus, copper and manganese, high-fibre barley can also give your intestinal health a boost. Hulled barley has more fibre than pearl barley, which is polished to remove the fibrous bran. Besides this robust risotto, barley can be added to soups and stews and also to baked goods.

Be Organic – Savvy

Whether you're keen to be more environmentally friendly; want to avoid chemical additives, such as pesticides, in your food; or simply want to aim for better overall wellbeing, then going organic, when possible, can have proven health benefits for you and your family.

Organic food is grown naturally without the use, or with very minimal use, of harmful chemicals. People may wonder if organic food really is better for them. My view is this: even if organic food was proven to have no greater nutritional value than standard crops, the fact that it is not treated with toxic fertilisers and pesticides means it's got to be better for us.

Why Choose Organic Food?

* Organic food simply tastes better — it tastes like food used to taste.
* Organic food is, in my opinion, more wholesome and nutritious.
* It's safer not to eat foods treated with pesticides and other chemicals.
* It means avoiding genetically altered foods. Organic foods are not manipulated but left to grow as nature intended.
* Organic production methods and farming practices are better for the environment, having less impact on soil, waterways, eco-systems and the planet.

I'm not demanding everyone must buy only organic, but if what I've said here encourages you to at least try some organic alternatives, then this is a great step in the right direction. I'm sure once you get started you will find organics can enhance your health and your life. Here are some good reasons for a change to organics and some tips to help you make the transition.

A good way to get hold of organic produce is to grow your own (see Start a Kitchen Garden, page 50). If this is not possible, then buying direct from producers, such as organic farmers' and growers' markets, is the next best thing. Buying from growers or specialised greengrocers, fishmongers and butchers can help you purchase the freshest seasonal produce — often at lower prices than supermarkets. You may find there's more variety on offer too.

Buying organic fruits and vegetables through a box-delivery scheme is another good method. Mixed produce is packed into boxes and delivered to your door, and often delivery costs can be quite low. Fruits and vegetables start to lose their flavour and nutritional value the moment they're picked. By sharing boxes of produce with friends, you can place orders more regularly and make sure your supply is constant and always super fresh.

Organically reared animals are not given hormones or antibiotics and they thrive on a natural diet of organic feed to produce healthy meat. I have consciously not included any red meat recipes in this book, only because I want to showcase the delicious versatility of vegetables, grains and pulses. Also, in the interests of health and variety, many people have recognised the sense of eating less red meat each week. So, I have included some recipes for tasty, light fish and chicken dishes, to help people make this transition with ease.

Interestingly, eating more fruit and vegetables often proves to be not just a healthier option but a more economical practice, too. Compared to meat, seafood and cheese, fruit, vegetables, grains and pulses are much less expensive. A clever technique is to incorporate dairy products, meat, poultry and fish in your cooking as minor ingredients rather than the main ingredient in a dish, just as they do in Mediterranean and Asian cuisines, well known for their healthy, balanced diets.

Go Natural

One of the best things we can do is to cut down on processed foods. Choose natural and organic products, when you can, as eating real food is a great way to feel, look and be healthier. Certified organic products are real food, as they have been made using only organic ingredients, without additives such as preservatives, flavour enhancers and colourings.

Making your own meals from natural ingredients and home baking means you know exactly what has gone into the food you and your family are eating. Having your kitchen stocked with healthy, fresh food will help you to make better meal choices and keep it natural.

> "Buying from growers or specialised greengrocers, fishmongers and butchers can help you purchase the freshest seasonal produce."

Food Sensitivities

Food sensitivities are becoming increasingly common and can cause symptoms ranging from constant headaches, hay fever and mild flu-like conditions, to bloating and fatigue. Some people develop a sensitivity or intolerance to certain foods, such as wheat, dairy products, soy and nuts, causing them to have an allergic reaction. Allergic reactions can be extreme, for example, for those with nut allergies a single peanut can cause anaphylactic shock and even death.

Wheat and other grains contain a protein called

gluten. Gluten is difficult for some people to digest and can cause mild to severe digestive problems. At the extreme end of this intolerance lies coeliac (celiac) disease, which is a severe auto-immune condition that destroys the lining of the small intestine, and in doing so disrupts nutrient absorption.

Some people develop sensitivities because of over-consumption of a food, such as dairy products or gluten. Sometimes there are potential allergens in foods we might not expect to find them in. For example, soy sauce contains wheat and therefore gluten. Soy, gluten and corn are in a huge number of processed foods and some unexpected foods may have traces of peanuts. This is why it's wise to read food labels carefully (see page 201).

Many people initially find food sensitivities and intolerances hard to cater for. At first it might be hard to find good, reliable recipes for dishes, and especially baking, that still taste good. That's why I've included a lot of delicious gluten-free recipes in this book, as well as some dairy-free alternatives for those who need them.

It is important to realise that any baking made without gluten will have a completely different texture to what you may be used to. This is not a bad thing, just different. Depending on the recipe, expect some gluten-free cakes to have a crumblier texture because gluten usually gives baking structure and holds things together. Some baking, such as breads and pastry, may be heavier than versions containing gluten. Once you get used to the difference though, and armed with good recipes, you will find gluten-free baking can be uniquely delicious.

Make Your Own Natural Baking Powder

The main ingredients of baking powder are cream of tartar and baking soda (also know as bicarbonate of soda or sodium bicarbonate). However, some purchased baking powders contain the chemical phosphate, which is used as an acid reactor. Cream of tartar is a natural substance that is a by-product created during winemaking, and baking soda is also a natural substance that is a mined mineral deposit called trona ore.

These two ingredients have been combined and used successfully in baking for decades, so there's really no need to add any unnecessary chemicals or gluten (which is also sometimes added) to this raising agent. It's really easy to make your own baking powder and I find this mixture has the best results of all. Here's how: simply measure two parts cream of tartar to one part baking soda, sift together and store in an airtight jar.

Light and Fragrant

low-fat options and portable feasts

✳ **Lighten up!** It's time to compose simple, satisfying meals that boost energy levels. Because what we eat matters, I've made these dishes appealingly full of fresh ingredients, high in taste impact and low in fat. Use these recipes to help you make simple lifestyle changes and enhance your everyday wellbeing.

Some of these recipes are lighter in another sense – they're lightweight and easy to transport. The wonderful thing about portable food is that it's not meant to be complex, so it's easy to pack your picnic basket with one of these tasty dishes and head off to enjoy the good life.

Moroccan Fish Tagine

Tagine cooking is very popular, however, if you don't own a tagine (conical-shaped Moroccan cooking pot) you can simply use a casserole dish or large, lidded frying-pan instead. This tasty fish dish contains all the flavours of the sun and works well with any firm-fleshed white fish.

SERVES 4   DF | EF | GF | WF

2 tbsp olive oil

1 large red onion, sliced

150 g button mushrooms, quartered

1 red capsicum, seeds removed, finely sliced

2 cloves garlic, chopped

1 tsp ground cumin

2 tsp ground coriander

½ tsp dried chilli flakes

400-g can chopped organic tomatoes

½ cup cold filtered water

600 g firm, white-fleshed fish, cut into 3-cm cubes

1 tbsp fresh lemon juice

salt and freshly ground black pepper

flesh of 1 preserved lemon, rinsed and finely chopped

2 tbsp chopped fresh coriander

2 tbsp chopped fresh parsley

Herbed Moroccan couscous (recipe follows), optional

1. Heat a tagine base or large frying-pan, add oil, onion, mushrooms and red capsicum strips and cook over medium–low heat for 10 minutes, stirring regularly until vegetables have softened but not browned.

2. Add garlic, cumin, coriander and chilli to pan and cook for 30 seconds more. Add canned tomatoes and any juice and the water. Bring mixture to the boil.

3. Now add cubed fish. Cover pan with lid (or use foil, if necessary) and turn down heat to gently simmer for 5–10 minutes, or until fish is just cooked.

4. Sprinkle dish with lemon juice and season with a little salt and pepper to taste. Scatter with the chopped preserved lemon, coriander and parsley. Serve as a one-pot meal or with herbed Moroccan couscous on the side, if desired.

✳ Natural selection . . . Excess sodium in the diet is linked to high blood pressure, so work towards reducing added salt in cooking. To give flavour to foods and reduce the need for salt, use lots of tasty ingredients in dishes, such as herbs, citrus zest and juice, chilli and other aromatic spices. Adding flavoursome spices, herbs and citrus to seasonal foods means that the addition of salt can be kept to a minimum and foods will still taste great.

Herbed Moroccan Couscous

Often mistaken for a grain, North Africa's staple, couscous, is actually tiny pasta made from a mixture of semolina, flour and water that is rolled into pellets and dried. Couscous absorbs other flavours easily and makes a lovely light accompaniment to many meals.

SERVES 4   DF | EF

2 tbsp olive oil

1 small onion, finely diced

¾ cup liquid vegetable or chicken stock, as preferred

¾ cup couscous

½ cup chopped fresh herbs, such as parsley, basil, coriander

juice of 1 lemon

salt and freshly ground black pepper

1. Heat oil in a large saucepan, add onion and cook for 8 minutes to soften but not brown. Add stock and bring to the boil.

2. Add couscous, stir to combine and remove pan from the heat. Cover and leave to steam and soften for 10 minutes.

3. Fluff up couscous with a fork to separate grains. Stir through herbs and lemon juice and season with salt and pepper to taste.

Brown Rice Sushi Salad with Salmon and Pickled Ginger

Great salads are all about fresh ingredients and good combinations, united by an exciting dressing and tweaked to suit your own preferences. This salad is a play on the popular Japanese sushi rolls and is like a deconstructed version of this super-healthy dish. Be sure to make your own Japanese pickled ginger, as it's easy to do, tastes fantastic, and finishes this salad off perfectly.

SERVES 4   DF | EF | GF | WF | V

1 cup short-grain brown rice

300 g freshest quality salmon fillet, skin and bones removed

2 sheets nori seaweed, cut into short, thin strips

3 spring onions, finely sliced

1 red capsicum, seeds removed, very finely sliced

1 tbsp black sesame seeds

Japanese pickled ginger, to serve (recipe follows)

wheat-free tamari, to serve (optional)

wasabi paste, to serve (optional)

TAMARI AND WASABI DRESSING

1 tbsp sesame oil

2 tbsp mirin

2 tbsp wheat-free tamari

½ tsp wasabi paste

juice of 1 lemon

1. Cook brown rice in plenty of boiling water for 30 minutes. Drain well and set aside to cool.

2. Combine dressing ingredients and pour the dressing over cold rice. Toss well to coat.

3. Scatter rice onto a serving platter. Thinly slice fresh salmon and arrange slices over rice.

4. Scatter over nori seaweed, spring onions, capsicum and sesame seeds. Serve with Japanese pickled ginger on the side and extra tamari and wasabi, if desired.

* **Nori** . . . is a dark greenish-black type of edible seaweed, sold in dry, paper-thin sheets. Used primarily for sushi rolls, nori can also be cut or crumbled and used to garnish noodle or rice dishes.

* **Tamari** . . . is a mellow-flavoured, naturally fermented Japanese soy sauce. Most soy sauce contains wheat, so if you follow a gluten-free diet then look for wheat-free tamari.

Japanese Pickled Ginger

It is important to use young ginger root for this pickle, as it is more pliable than older ginger and naturally changes colour to a pretty pale pink when preserved in this way.

MAKES 1½ CUPS   DF | EF | GF | WF

300 g young fresh ginger root, peeled and very thinly sliced

2 tsp salt

1 cup rice vinegar

¾ cup white sugar

1. Place sliced ginger in a colander set over a bowl; sprinkle with salt and leave to drain for 1 hour.

2. Rinse and dry ginger slices with paper towels and place in a sterilised jar. Combine rice vinegar and sugar in a small saucepan and bring to the boil, stirring until sugar dissolves.

3. Pour hot liquid over ginger slices and set aside to cool. Seal the jar and store it in the fridge.

Wood-Ear Mushroom and Silken Tofu Broth

Good stock is an important foundation of any soup. Enjoy making your own when you have the time; however, prepared organic stocks are a good standby. Beware that purchased stocks may be quite salty, so adjust seasoning at the end of cooking to allow for this.

SERVES 4   DF | EF | GF | WF | V

20 g dried wood-ear mushrooms (available from Asian grocery stores)

6 cups liquid vegetable stock (or vegetable cooking water)

2-cm piece ginger, peeled and thinly sliced

3–4 tbsp miso paste

350-g block silken tofu, cut into 2-cm cubes

1 red chilli, seeds removed, finely sliced (optional)

1 bunch spring onions, finely sliced

¼ cup torn coriander leaves and/or young shoots

I. Place wood-ear mushrooms in a bowl, cover with boiling water and leave for 15 minutes to soak and soften. Remove mushrooms and cut into small chunks, discarding any hard stems. Strain the soaking liquid to remove any sediment.

2. At the same time, place stock and ginger in a large saucepan and bring to the boil, then turn down heat and simmer for 10 minutes to infuse flavours. Add chopped mushrooms and strained soaking liquid.

3. Add miso paste and cubed tofu and simmer for 2 minutes more to heat through. Add chilli to taste, if desired.

4. Serve garnished with spring onions and coriander.

✻ **Wood-ear mushrooms** . . . Wood-ear mushrooms are a common ingredient in Chinese soups and stir-fries and are often considered the 'meat among vegetables'. Adding a crunchy texture to dishes, these mushrooms readily take on the taste of other ingredients due to their spongy texture once rehydrated. Also highly valued by Chinese herbalists for their blood-thinning properties, wood-ear fungus is an inexpensive and highly nutritious source of protein, iron and vitamins.

Vietnamese Chicken Noodle Salad

A salad is always refreshing on a hot summer's day and this one is especially so, due to the combination of crunchy fresh vegetables and the distinctive hot and zingy flavours of the dressing.

SERVES 6 DF | EF | WF | GF

3 skinless chicken breasts, trimmed of excess fat

100 g rice vermicelli

2 large peeled carrots

1 small cucumber, trimmed

4–5 spring onions, finely sliced

⅓ cup fresh coriander leaves

¼ cup torn mint leaves (preferably Vietnamese mint)

¼ cup torn fresh basil leaves

Vietnamese dressing (recipe follows)

1. First poach chicken (this can be done the day before, if desired). Place chicken breasts in a saucepan and cover with cold filtered water. Bring just to the boil then turn down heat and simmer gently for 10–15 minutes, depending on size.
2. Remove chicken and liquid to a large bowl to cool to room temperature. Refrigerate to cool completely. Cooling chicken in liquid will mean chicken is moist and juicy. Once cold, shred or slice chicken flesh into bite-sized pieces. Reserve liquid as it can be used as chicken stock at a later date.
3. Cook rice vermicelli noodles in boiling water for 2–3 minutes or until translucent. Drain, rinse under cold water, then drain well again and set aside. Use a vegetable peeler to peel the carrots and cucumber into thin ribbons.
4. Combine all salad ingredients in a large bowl. Pour dressing over, toss well and serve.

Vietnamese Dressing

I usually make a double batch of this dressing and store it in the fridge. It lasts for up to two months and is great to have on hand to dress a variety of salads, seafood, chicken, Asian greens or noodle dishes.

MAKES ¾ CUP DF | EF | WF | GF

juice of 3–4 limes
2–3 tbsp wheat- and gluten-free tamari
2–3 tbsp grated palm sugar or soft brown sugar
2 tbsp fish sauce
2 tbsp cold filtered water
1 small red chilli, seeds removed, finely chopped

1. Place all ingredients in a screw-top jar and shake to combine until sugar has dissolved.
2. Taste and add more lime juice, soy sauce or sugar to give the dressing a balanced sweet, hot, sour and salty flavour.

✱ **Rice vermicelli noodles** . . . Rice vermicelli noodles are made from rice flour and so are a great gluten-free alternative. Cut in ultra thin strips and sold dried, you will find these noodles in supermarkets or Asian grocery stores. With little taste of their own, rice vermicelli noodles will readily take on other flavours and are great for tossing with extra tasty ingredients, such as lime, chilli and soy sauce.

Raw Energy Salad Platter with Avocado Salsa

This salad is a very tasty example of a 'raw food' recipe. Some people choose to follow a completely raw food diet because cooking can diminish the nutritional value of food and they want all the benefits that living food gives them. Raw food enthusiasts report increased energy, better bodily functions and vibrant good health. Enjoying just a few uncooked meals each week can bring immediate changes, making you feel cleansed and revitalised.

SERVES 4   DF | EF | GF | WF | V

- -

I large beetroot, peeled and grated

finely grated zest and juice of 1 lemon

I tbsp cold-pressed sesame oil

salt and freshly ground black pepper

2 courgettes, grated

¼ cup chopped fresh parsley

2 large carrots, peeled and grated

I bunch radishes, grated

I tbsp rosewater

½ cup pea shoots or bean sprouts

¼ cup sunflower seeds

¼ cup pumpkin seeds

2 tbsp flax seeds

2 tbsp sesame seeds

½ cup whole almonds, coarsely chopped

I cup rocket leaves

Avocado salsa (recipe follows)

- -

I. Place grated beetroot in a bowl. Sprinkle with lemon juice and oil and toss well. Season with salt and pepper to taste.

2. Combine grated courgettes with the chopped parsley and lemon zest. Season with salt and pepper to taste.

3. Combine the grated carrots and radishes. Drizzle with rosewater and season with salt and pepper to taste.

4. Arrange the separate salad components on a platter, or on individual plates. Sprinkle with seeds and nuts and garnish with rocket leaves. Serve with avocado salsa on the side, to spoon over.

Avocado Salsa

With a creamy texture and vibrant flavours, this raw avocado salsa can also be served as a dip for fresh vegetable sticks (crudités).

MAKES 1 CUP   DF | EF | GF | WF | V

1 avocado

juice of 2 limes (or 1 lemon)

½ small red onion, finely diced

1 small red chilli, seeds removed, finely diced

¼ cup chopped fresh coriander

salt and freshly ground black pepper

1. Cut avocado in half and remove stone. Scoop out flesh with a spoon. Finely dice flesh and place in a bowl. Immediately squeeze over lime juice to prevent avocado from turning brown.

2. Add remaining ingredients. Season with salt and pepper and toss well.

- -

* Raw foods . . . When we talk about 'raw foods', we mean edible plants in their natural, unprocessed, uncooked state, including: fruit and vegetables, seeds, nuts, grains and legumes in sprouted form, and seaweeds. As well as tasting fresh and clean, raw foods contain a wide range of essential nutrients and live enzymes, antioxidants and are incredibly high in fibre.

Edible Rainbow Salad Baskets with Lemony Mustard Dressing

Different-coloured foods contain different nutrients, and that's why it's important to eat a range of colours each day for optimum health. This energising raw food salad comprises a veritable rainbow of fresh foods.

SERVES 6 EF

SALAD BASKETS

6 Mexican soft flour tortillas
olive oil spray
½ small red cabbage, finely shredded
1 cup bean sprouts
1 red capsicum, seeds removed, thinly sliced
2 sticks celery, cut into thin strips
3 spring onions, cut into thin strips
2 peeled carrots, cut into thin strips
150 g raw green beans, chopped
¼ cup chopped fresh parsley

LEMONY MUSTARD DRESSING

juice of 2 lemons
1 tsp honey
1 tbsp wholegrain mustard
3 tbsp extra virgin olive oil
freshly ground black pepper to taste

OPTIONAL TOPPINGS

100 g feta, cubed or crumbled
185-g can tuna in spring water, drained
  and flaked
torn fresh basil leaves, to garnish

1. Preheat oven to 180 °C. Lightly spray tortillas on both sides with oil. Push one tortilla into each hole of a 6-hole Texas muffin tin to form baskets — cutting them down a little to fit, if necessary.

2. Bake baskets for 10 minutes or until golden brown and crispy. Remove to cool in the tin.

3. Make salad by combining all ingredients in a large bowl.

4. In a small bowl, whisk all the dressing ingredients together. Pour dressing over salad and toss well to combine. Pack the salad into the crisp tortilla baskets. Top with either crumbled feta or canned tuna, if desired. Garnish with torn basil leaves.

5. If transporting to a picnic site, to avoid the baskets going soggy, it's advisable to transport the salad, dressing and basket components separately. Then, simply dress the salad and fill the baskets on-site, just before eating.

✱ **Tortillas** . . . A Mexican staple, tortillas are unleavened, flat breads made from either flour or cornmeal. Tortillas can be eaten raw and are often used as a wrapping for salads and other fillings. When baked, tortillas become firm and crisp (like tortilla crisps) and make an ideal basket for filling with salad.

Aromatic Chicken Filo Parcels

Filo pastry is traditionally brushed with copious amounts of butter. However, in this recipe, I've opted for a little healthy oil instead to make these chicken parcels delightfully light on fat. Fat, however, does lend richness and flavour to food, so if you're removing fat from cooking then you may need to increase the seasoning by adding some flavour-enhancing ingredients, such as fresh herbs, sultry spices, fragrant seeds, aromatic vinegars and other tasty condiments — just as I've done with these tasty parcels.

MAKES 6

1 tbsp olive oil
1 onion, finely diced
400 g lean chicken mince
2 cloves garlic, chopped
2 tsp fennel seeds
400-g can chopped organic tomatoes
2 tbsp tomato paste
½ cup chopped stuffed green olives

finely grated zest of 1 lemon
3 tbsp chopped fresh parsley
1 tbsp chopped fresh oregano
salt and freshly ground black pepper
9 sheets filo pastry
olive oil spray
1 tbsp caraway seeds
2 tbsp sesame seeds

1. Heat oil in a saucepan, add onion and chicken mince and cook over medium heat for 10 minutes until onion is softened and mince lightly browned. Add garlic and fennel seeds and cook for 1 minute more.
2. Add tomatoes and any juice and tomato paste and cook over medium heat for 10–15 minutes until liquid is well reduced. Stir in olives, lemon zest and herbs and season with salt and pepper to taste. Set mixture aside to cool completely.
3. Preheat oven to 200 °C. Working quickly, spray one sheet of filo lightly with oil. Place a second sheet on top, spray with oil and place a third sheet on top. Cut layered sheets of filo in half to give two squares. Repeat with remaining sheets of filo so that you have six squares of three layers each.
4. Divide the cold chicken mince mixture by six and place a portion in the centre of each filo square. Bring the corners of one square together and twist in the centre to secure the filling. Repeat with remaining squares to form six parcels.
5. Place parcels on a baking tray. Lightly spray the outside of the parcels with oil and scatter with caraway and sesame seeds. Bake for 15–20 minutes or until crisp and golden brown all over.

Fragrant Rice Picnic Pies

Made with fragrant basmati rice, these pies are light yet wonderfully tasty. The whole tomatoes not only look attractive sitting prettily on top of each pie, but they also act like an instant sauce-bomb that explodes when cut, adding even more flavour to these picnic pies.

SERVES 6   GF | WF

½ cup basmati rice
3 spring onions, chopped
2 large courgettes, coarsely grated
2 tbsp chopped fresh basil
100 g cow's or goat's milk feta, crumbled

4 eggs
½ cup low-fat milk (or substitute rice milk, if preferred)
salt and freshly ground black pepper
6 small vine-ripened tomatoes

1. Preheat oven to 180 °C. Line a 6-hole Texas muffin tin with squares of non-stick baking paper, cut to fit so that the paper comes right up the sides of each tin.

2. Cook rice in plenty of boiling water for 12 minutes. Drain well and rinse with cold water to cool. Drain well and transfer to a bowl. Add spring onions and grated courgettes to cooled rice. Stir in basil and feta.

3. In a separate bowl, beat eggs together with the milk, and then stir into the rice mixture. Season well with salt and pepper.

4. Spoon mixture into prepared tins, dividing it evenly. Top each with a tomato, pressed halfway into mixture. Bake for 30–40 minutes or until firm and set.

✳ Keep it light . . . Choose a lightweight, yet sturdy, hamper to transport your moveable feast with ease. Keep it simple; don't pack unnecessary items that can make the hamper heavy and difficult to carry. It's a good idea to carry fragile foods, like freshly baked pies and tarts, in the tins they were baked in so they don't get knocked around during transportation.

Salmon Terrine

It is possible to use breadcrumbs made from gluten-free bread in this recipe —
simply substitute measure for measure.

SERVES 8

olive oil, to grease tin
¼ cup dry breadcrumbs (can be made from
   gluten-free bread)
500 g skinless fresh salmon fillet, bones
   removed
1 medium onion, coarsely chopped
1 medium carrot, coarsely grated
finely grated zest and juice of 1 lemon

½ cup low-fat plain unsweetened yoghurt
1 cup fresh breadcrumbs (can be made from
   gluten-free bread)
2 eggs
salt and freshly ground black pepper
extra low-fat sour cream, to serve
fresh rocket leaves, to serve
lemon wedges, to serve

1. Preheat oven to 170 °C. Lightly brush or spray a 1.5-litre capacity loaf
tin with oil and then sprinkle with the dry breadcrumbs to coat, reserving
2 tablespoons.

2. Cut salmon into coarse chunks. Place salmon and remaining ingredients in
the bowl of a food processor and process to combine into a smooth mixture.
Season with salt and pepper to taste.

3. Spread mixture into prepared loaf tin, packing it in well and smoothing
surface with the back of a spoon. Sprinkle reserved dry breadcrumbs over the
surface.

4. Bake for 60 minutes or until firm. Slice to serve warm. Alternatively,
refrigerate until cold and transport to a picnic site, if desired. Serve with a
dollop of sour cream, some rocket leaves and with lemon wedges on the side,
to squeeze over.

* My advice . . . For heart health, reduce saturated fats, which can increase the
risk of heart disease. When possible, choose low-fat versions of ingredients, such as
yoghurt, sour cream, mayonnaise or coconut milk, as these contain much less fat
than standard forms.

Extra Virgin Olive Oil

The Good Oil

Fat is a big topic, in more ways than one. Some fats are essential for our good health and wellbeing, while others can be detrimental.

All living cells contain fat. Fat is important for brain function, to insulate nerve cells, protect organs, create hormones, lubricate joints, keep our skin and arteries supple, keep us warm and give us energy. Fat also allows us to absorb the fat-soluble vitamins A, D, E and K.

In the kitchen, fat can add great aroma, texture and flavour to food. However, it's important that we choose the right kinds of fat, and consume the right quantities.

Saturated and Unsaturated

It's wise to limit saturated fats in your diet, as these are harder to digest and too much can raise cholesterol and increase the risk of heart disease. Saturated fats are predominantly found in animal products, such as meat and dairy products. Tropical oils, such as palm oil and coconut butter, are also high in saturated fats. Unsaturated fats can help lower cholesterol and are also packed with nutrients. Excellent choices include olive oil, avocado, fresh nuts and seeds, and oily fish such as salmon, mackerel and sardines.

Trans Fats

You will want to avoid unhealthy trans fats, especially when you understand more about them. Trans fats are toxic, manufactured fats, created through a process called hydrogenation, where oils are stabilised to keep them solid at room temperature and to stop rancidity. Found in processed foods, fast foods, fried foods, commercial baked goods and margarines, trans fats have been found to increase risks of heart disease and certain cancers.

Alternatives

If you must use an alternative to butter, I suggest you choose unhydrogenated dairy-free spreads, or olive oil. I want to mention an amazing cooking fat that I like to use for Indian curries and some Asian stir-fries: ghee, also known as clarified butter. Ghee is pure butter fat with the protein milk solids and water removed. It has an extremely high smoke point and will not oxidise and turn rancid or toxic at high temperatures.

Popular in North Indian cooking, ghee is also used in the practice of natural Indian medicine. The fatty acids in ghee have antioxidant and anti-inflammatory properties and can lower cholesterol, so it can be good for your heart. It's easy to make your own ghee. Simply melt butter until liquid, and then skim off any foam from the surface. Pour off and reserve the liquid yellow butter fat (this is ghee) and discard the white milk solids and sediment. Store ghee in a covered jar in the fridge.

Because fat adds flavour to food, if you're removing much of the fat from cooking then you will want to add some natural flavour-enhancing ingredients. Here are some tasty examples: use lots of fresh herbs, as herbs contain essential oils that add strong flavour and goodness to food. Orange, lemon or lime zest and juice can infuse meals with a real zing. Spices add vibrant aroma and richness to seafood, meat and vegetable dishes, dressings and marinades and also desserts.

Cold-pressed avocado oil and nut oils, such as macadamia, almond and walnut oils are also healthy options and these add great flvour and goodness to food. Grapeseed oil is a natural antioxidant and of course a source of Vitamin E. Its subtle flavour makes it ideal for baking and its high smoke point makes it a good choice for frying.

Olive Oil

When you do need oil for cooking, use good-quality olive oil. Not only does olive oil have wonderful flavour but it has many health benefits, too. Olive oil is rich in monounsaturated fats that help reduce unhealthy cholesterol and encourage the good cholesterol in our blood. Olive oil contains natural antioxidants that assist in protecting us against disease; and essential omega-3

"In the kitchen, fat can add a great aroma, texture and flavour to food. However, it's important that we choose the right kinds of fat, and consume the right quantities"

fatty acids, which our bodies can't produce naturally so we must get from food sources.

Based on my personal research, I have come to the conclusion that the only oil I want to cook with and eat is natural olive oil. Olive oil may have a lower smoke point than some other oils (the smoke point is used as a marker for when the oil starts to decompose and is reached when a visible smoky vapour starts to rise from hot oil), however, studies have shown that olive oil does not rapidly oxidise when the heat goes up and that hydrogenation occurs to a lesser degree than in other oils. You see, it all starts to get very technical, suffice it to say that olive oil is the healthiest oil, so why not leave the details to science and just enjoy it!

More About the Good Stuff

Olive oil really is the good oil — it not only tastes good but it is actually really good for us. Made by pressing ripe olives, the fruit of the evergreen olive tree, olive oil is quite literally the juice of olives. Completely natural, olive oil is a great tasting and heart-healthy oil with many positive health benefits. Olive oil is a monounsaturated fat high in essential fatty acids known to help reduce unhealthy blood-cholesterol levels and also containing high levels of vitamin E, antioxidants and anti-inflammatory compounds. Olive oil has been used in cooking for thousands of years and forms the basis of the famously healthy Mediterranean diet, which has particularly low levels of heart disease.

Ranging in flavour from mild and fruity, mellow and buttery, green and grassy, to richly exotic and peppery, olive oil has many uses from dipping, baking and pan-frying to salad dressings and marinades. Light and heat can cause olive oil to turn rancid, so it is best to buy oil in tinted bottles or cans. It is best stored in a cool, dark place, out of direct heat and sunlight.

Not all olive oils are created equal and it's good to know what to look for and how to understand the details on the bottle's labels. Here are some guidelines:

* Extra virgin olive oil (EVOO) is the highest quality, most nutrient-dense and flavourful olive oil. Virgin means no heat or chemical treatment has been used. EVOO is made from the first cold-pressing of the olives and contains powerful antioxidants called polyphenols. Not refining the oil has the benefit of safeguarding its vital nutrients and healthy properties. This oil is on the list of the world's healthiest foods.

* Quality unrefined EVOO is the best choice for adding flavour and goodness to finished dishes. Drizzle it over salads, cooked meats, poultry, shellfish, pasta or vegetables, or serve it with bread for dipping. However, it can also be used to cook foods.

* Virgin olive oil has less flavour and more acidity then extra virgin oil and is made from the second pressing of the olives. This oil can be used for pan-frying, roasting and grilling.

* Pure olive oil is a misnomer, as it actually refers to refined oil blended with virgin oil to add flavour. Refined oil is treated with chemicals to extract the oil. The refining process damages a lot of the fragile compounds responsible for olive oil's health benefits.

* Light olive oil is also a refined oil. In this case, the term 'light' refers to its mild taste and not any low-fat characteristics. It's possible to use light olive oil in baking, such as in muffins or cakes, as the flavour does not overpower these delicate goodies. However, I prefer to use a mild, fruit-flavoured virgin oil in my baking.

Natural Baking

deliciously natural baked treats

✱ There's something magical about the alchemy of eggs, sugar and flour, mixed with spices, cocoa, nuts or fruit that takes us back to a simpler time. If, like me, you also enjoy home baking for the sheer delight of the made-by-hand process, then this can be a wonderfully therapeutic pastime. The following recipes are part of my signature repertoire of baked delights - only, I've given them a makeover, so they're more natural. When I updated these recipes to be better for us than other sometime treats, I also made sure they retained their intrinsic charm and good taste.

Super Berry Cake

Delicious, super-healthy berries feature both inside
this yummy cake and also in the vibrant crushed
blueberry glaze.

SERVES 12

olive oil spray

2 cups unbleached spelt flour,
plus extra for dusting

2 large eggs

1 cup caster sugar

1 tsp pure vanilla extract

½ cup light olive oil

½ cup plain unsweetened
yoghurt

⅓ cup Craisins

1½ cups blueberries (fresh or
thawed from frozen)

1 tsp gluten-free baking powder

½ tsp baking soda

Blueberry crush glaze (recipe
follows)

1. Preheat oven to 160 °C fan bake. Lightly oil a 22-cm
bundt (special patterned tin) or ring cake tin and lightly
dust with flour. Place eggs, sugar, vanilla and oil in a bowl
and beat with an electric mixer until the mixture is pale
and sugar has dissolved.

2. Stir in yoghurt, Craisins and blueberries. Sift flour,
baking powder and soda over wet ingredients, then stir
just enough to combine.

3. Spoon mixture into prepared cake tin. Bake for 50
minutes, or until a skewer inserted comes out clean.
Remove to cool in the tin for 20 minutes to firm before
turning cake out onto a wire rack to cool completely.

4. Once cold, drizzle cake with blueberry crush glaze and
slice to serve.

Blueberry Crush Glaze

MAKES ⅔ CUP   DF | EF | GF | WF | V

¼ cup blueberries (fresh or defrosted
from frozen)

1 cup gluten-free icing sugar, sifted

2–3 tsp lemon juice

1. Purée blueberries with the icing sugar in a
small food processor.

2. Add just enough lemon juice to bring the
mixture to a slightly runny consistency.

* **Berries** . . . With more antioxidant
power than most other fruits, blueberries
and cranberries strengthen our body
tissue defences against oxidation and
inflammation. Inflammation is thought
to be a key driver of chronic diseases,
so these berries hold a stack of benefits.

Chocolate Courgette Cake

This is a wonderfully rustic kind of cake that has a dense, moist texture similar to steamed pudding. I like it plain but it can be tarted up with a delicious honey cream cheese frosting, and decorated with chocolate, fruit and nuts, if desired. The recipe makes a large cake, but it lasts well if stored in an airtight container in the fridge.

SERVES 16   DF | GF | WF

olive oil spray
tapioca flour, for dusting
3 small eggs
1 cup raw sugar
2 tbsp honey
¾ cup light olive oil
2 tsp pure vanilla extract
2 cups (about 3 medium-sized) firmly packed grated courgettes
½ cup chopped walnuts

½ cup Craisins
1 cup buckwheat flour
⅓ cup cocoa powder
pinch of salt
1 tbsp ground cinnamon
1 tsp gluten-free baking powder
1 tsp baking soda
Honey cream cheese fruit-nut frosting (recipe follows, optional)

1. Preheat oven to 160 °C fan bake. Spray a 22-cm bundt (special patterned tin) or ring cake tin with oil and then lightly dust with tapioca flour.

2. Place eggs, sugar, honey, oil and vanilla in a bowl and beat until mixture is pale and sugar has dissolved. Stir in grated courgettes, walnuts and Craisins.

3. Sift buckwheat flour, cocoa, salt, cinnamon, baking powder and soda over the courgette mixture and stir to combine.

4. Pour mixture into prepared tin and bake for 60–70 minutes or until cake tests cooked when a skewer inserted in the centre comes out moist but clean. Set aside to cool in the tin for 30 minutes, then invert onto a wire rack to cool completely.

5. Serve plain, or spread with honey cream cheese fruit-nut frosting and decorate, if desired.

Honey Cream Cheese Fruit-Nut Frosting

MAKES ½ CUP   EF | GF | WF

I love the taste of cream cheese frosting, but not the high fat content. So, after some experimentation, I've came up with this simple combination that still tastes great and satisfies my craving for a yummy creamy frosting, without all that fat and sugar.

125 g cream cheese, at room temperature
1 tbsp strong-flavoured honey
2 tbsp chopped dark chocolate
2 tbsp chopped whole almonds
2 tbsp Craisins

1. In a bowl, beat cream cheese until smooth. Add honey and beat to combine.

2. Spoon frosting over cold cake and decorate with chopped chocolate, almonds and Craisins.

✱ **Cocoa** . . . Cocoa is super high in antioxidants and contains an array of minerals, so it's a good idea to use natural cocoa powder as a base flavour for your chocolate baking, like in this cake.

Celebration Fruit Cake

Most traditional-style fruit cakes need time to develop flavour and texture — that's why they're usually made well in advance of any special occasion. This cake, however, is best made and eaten within four weeks, due to the fact that it contains no gluten or dairy. The beauty of this last-minute type of fruit cake is that it still has a great depth of flavour and slices perfectly, even when freshly made.

MAKES AN 18 CM SQUARE CAKE   DF | GF | WF

300 g sultanas
300 g raisins
300 g currants
100 g Craisins
⅔ cup firmly packed dark cane sugar
2 tbsp treacle
2 tbsp orange marmalade
1 cup orange juice
⅔ cup light olive oil
4 large eggs, lightly beaten

½ cup ground almonds
1 cup buckwheat flour
½ cup tapioca flour
½ tsp gluten-free baking powder
1 tbsp cocoa powder
1 tbsp cinnamon
1 tsp ground ginger
½ tsp ground cloves
½ cup whole almonds, to decorate

1. Place dried fruits, sugar, treacle, marmalade, orange juice and oil in a saucepan. Bring mixture just to the boil and then turn down the heat and simmer very gently for 10 minutes. Remove pan from heat. Transfer mixture to a large bowl and set aside to cool to room temperature.

2. Preheat oven to 140 °C. Line base and sides of a 20-cm square cake tin with a double thickness of baking paper.

3. Stir beaten eggs into the cooled fruit mixture. Stir in ground almonds. Sift flours, baking powder, cocoa and spices over the mixture and then stir just enough to combine. Spread mixture into the prepared cake tin. Scatter the cake's surface randomly with whole almonds to decorate.

4. Bake for 3 hours or until a skewer inserted in the centre of the cake comes out clean. Leave to cool in the tin. This cake will last well for 3–4 weeks, if stored in an airtight container in a cool place. Or store in the fridge during hot weather.

✻ **Baking savvy** . . . Store rich fruit cakes wrapped in greaseproof paper (never plastic wrap, as this will cause the cake to sweat and deteriorate more rapidly) and then wrap in several layers of newspaper (which allows the cake to breathe). If the cake is to be kept for some weeks, it is a good idea to 'feed' it with alcohol, such as whiskey or brandy to help preserve it. To do this, pierce the cake all over with a skewer and then drizzle with your chosen spirit. Repeat several times over the weeks.

Individual Chocolate Brownie Cakes

Generously loaded with chocolate flavour and with a rich, dense texture, these brownies are fudgy and delicious, just as the best brownies should be. However, this recipe just happens to be wheat- and gluten-free, into the bargain. For a variation, I've suggested dividing the mixture between small cake tins to make individual brownies. I like it this way, as individual servings give a higher ratio of crunchy outside texture. However, the mixture can be made in a brownie tin and sliced, too, if preferred. Whichever way you choose, these brownies are definite crowd pleasers.

MAKES 12   GF | WF

100 g butter, melted and cooled
½ cup good-quality cocoa powder
¼ cup tapioca flour
½ tsp gluten-free baking powder
1 cup firmly packed brown sugar

2 eggs, lightly beaten
1 tsp pure vanilla extract
½ cup coarsely chopped good-quality dark chocolate (or gluten-free chocolate chips)
extra cocoa powder, for dusting

1. Preheat oven to 160 °C. Grease 12 x 100-ml-capacity cake or muffin tins and line the bases with circles of baking paper, cut to fit.

2. Sift cocoa, flour and baking powder into a bowl. Stir in sugar and make a well in the centre. Pour cooled melted butter, beaten eggs and vanilla extract into the well. Stir just enough to combine. Stir in chopped chocolate or chocolate chips.

3. Spoon mixture into prepared tins, dividing it evenly. Bake brownies for 25 minutes, or until a skewer inserted into the centre of one cake comes out moist but clean.

4. Remove brownies to cool in the tins then turn out. Serve dusted with extra cocoa, if desired.

5. Stored in an airtight container, separating layers with greaseproof paper, brownies will last well for 3–4 days.

6. Alternatively, if you want to add something extra to the mix, stir in half a cup of toasted nuts, such as almonds, walnuts or pecans. Or, add half a cup of raisins or Craisins before baking.

✽   **Kitchen savvy** . . . To keep chocolate chunks or chips whole in baked goods, such as these brownies, make sure that the cake batter is cold (that is, the melted butter has cooled) before stirring in the chocolate chips, otherwise the chips will melt into the cake mixture and not retain their shape.

Chocolate Date Truffles

MAKES 24   GF | WF

½ cup cream
200 g good-quality dark eating chocolate, coarsely chopped
⅓ cup chopped pitted dates
½ cup coarsely grated dark chocolate, chocolate flakes or sprinkles

1. Place cream in a heatproof bowl and microwave for 2 minutes until almost boiling, or heat in a saucepan, then transfer to a bowl.
2. Add chopped chocolate and set aside for a few minutes to melt. Stir until smooth. Stir in chopped dates. Leave mixture to cool completely then cover and chill for at least 1 hour, or overnight.
3. Roll mixture into small balls (about a heaped tablespoonful) to make truffles. Spread the grated chocolate out on a dinner plate and roll the truffles in the flakes to coat. Truffles last well for up to a week if covered and stored in the fridge.

✳ **Dates** . . . Dates are a great source of natural fibre and rich in vitamins and minerals that are key to good health. Packed with easily digested natural sugars, carbohydrates and fibre, dates are a perfect energy-boosting snack.

Date and Apple Cakelets

MAKES 8   DF | EF | GF | WF | V

200 g chopped pitted dates
¼ cup honey
½ cup apple juice
olive oil spray
1 cooking apple, grated with skin on
½ cup ground almonds
1 tsp pure vanilla extract
⅓ cup buckwheat flour
1 tsp gluten-free baking powder
¼ cup flaked almonds

1. Place dates and honey in a bowl. Heat apple juice and pour over dates. Set aside for one hour for dates to soften and cool.
2. Preheat oven to 160 °C. Lightly oil eight standard muffin tins or line with paper cases.
3. Stir grated apple, ground almonds and vanilla into the cooked date mixture. Stir in sifted flour and baking powder.
4. Spoon mixture into prepared tins. Sprinkle each with flaked almonds. Bake for 45 minutes.

Nutty Date and Ginger Bars

MAKES 24   DF | GF | WF

2 eggs
¾ cup firmly packed dark cane sugar
1 tsp pure vanilla extract
¾ cup gluten-free self-raising flour, sifted
400 g whole pitted dates
1 cup walnut pieces
½ cup chopped crystallised ginger

1. Preheat oven to 180 °C. Line a 17 x 27-cm slice tin with non-stick baking paper, leaving an overhang on all sides. In a bowl, beat eggs, sugar and vanilla for 5 minutes until pale and fluffy.
2. Gently fold in sifted flour. Fold in whole dates, walnuts and crystallised ginger, just enough to combine.
3. Spoon mixture into prepared tin and spread out to cover evenly. Bake for 35–40 minutes or until firm and golden brown.
4. Set aside to cool in the tin then remove by using the paper overhang to lift out the slab. Slice into squares or bars to serve.

Sesame Date Bliss Balls

MAKES 20   DF | EF | GF | WF | V

½ cup chopped pitted dates
½ cup raisins
½ cup chopped dried apricots
2 tbsp flax seeds
1 cup walnuts or almonds
1 tsp each ground ginger and cinnamon
¼ cup honey
½ cup sesame seeds

1. Place dates, raisins, apricots, flax seeds and nuts in the bowl of a food processor and process to mince. Add spices and process to combine – the mixture should be a thick, textured paste.
2. Warm honey in a small saucepan until liquid. Add honey to ground fruit and nut mixture and process to combine.
3. Shape mixture into walnut-sized balls and place on a small tray. Chill for 1 hour or until firm. Roll bliss balls in sesame seeds to coat. They will keep for three weeks, stored in the fridge.

Birdseed Bars

A slice is a baked goodie made in a slab pan. It's a crossbreed — more dense than a biscuit but less substantial than cake. I'm a big fan of sweet slices — they're infinitely versatile, easy to cut and serve, and perfect to fill a gap and lift your spirits any time of the day. This elegant play on a retro favourite makes a divine treat with your morning coffee and a healthy snack for children. Or, cut in tiny squares, this slice can be served after dinner, as a sweetmeat.

MAKES 18   EF | WF

90 g butter, cubed
½ cup firmly packed dark cane sugar
½ cup honey
2½ cups old-fashioned rolled oats
1 cup chopped walnuts or almonds

1 cup raisins
¼ cup sesame seeds
¼ cup sunflower seeds
¼ cup pumpkin seeds
¼ cup flax seeds

1. Preheat oven to 170 °C. Line a 17 x 27-cm slice tin with non-stick baking paper, leaving an overhang on all sides. Place butter, sugar and honey in a saucepan and heat until melted but don't boil.

2. Combine remaining ingredients in a large bowl. Pour melted mixture over dry ingredients and stir to combine.

3. Spoon mixture into prepared tin, pressing it down well with the back of a spoon to compact. Bake for 45 minutes or until golden brown.

4. Cool in the tin then remove by using the paper overhang to lift out the slab. Slice into small bars or squares to serve. Store in an airtight container.

✱ **Kitchen savvy** . . . When lining the tin with baking paper, leave an overhang of paper on all sides. The extra paper serves a dual purpose: it prevents the slice from sticking to the tin, of course, but it also provides nifty handles that enable you to magically lift the whole slice out of the tin in one easy movement.

Carrot Cake Cookies

Carrots have a high natural sugar content, so are perfect as the main player in this cookie recipe. Packed full of chunks of carrot and nuts, and with an aftertaste of lemon juice icing, these cookies are sure to become firm favourites in your household.

MAKES 24   DF | WF

⅓ cup light olive oil
½ cup firmly packed dark cane
    sugar
1 tsp pure vanilla extract
1 large egg
finely grated zest of 1 lemon
1 cup (2 medium-sized) firmly
    packed grated carrots
½ cup Craisins
⅓ cup chopped toasted walnuts

1 cup spelt flour, sifted
½ tsp baking powder
pinch of salt
1 tsp ground cinnamon
½ cup old-fashioned rolled oats
1 tbsp desiccated coconut
Lemon juice glaze (recipe
    follows)
extra walnut pieces, to decorate

Lemon Juice Glaze

Containing only two ingredients and no fat, you'll be thrilled with the intense taste of this simple glaze.

MAKES ½ CUP   DF | EF | GF | WF | V

1 cup icing sugar
2–3 tbsp lemon juice

1. Beat just enough lemon juice into the icing sugar to form a spreadable consistency.

1. Preheat oven to 180 °C. Line two baking sheets with non-stick baking paper. Place oil, sugar, vanilla and egg in a bowl and beat for 1 minute to combine.

2. Stir in lemon zest, grated carrots, Craisins and walnuts to combine. Add flour, baking powder, salt, cinnamon, rolled oats and coconut and stir to just combine.

3. Place slightly heaped tablespoonfuls of the mixture on the prepared baking sheets. Bake for 12–15 minutes or until golden brown. Remove to a wire rack to cool.

4. Once cold, top with a tablespoonful of lemon juice glaze and decorate each cookie with a walnut piece.

✳ **Cranberries and Craisins** . . . The important healthy properties of cranberries and Craisins survive the cooking process, which makes them a stand-out ingredient and great for use in all sorts of different recipes. That's why I've added yummy Craisins to these cookies.

Fruity Tea Loaf

I've always been a big fan of fruit loaves. This lovely version has a wonderful perfume that comes from the herbal tea infusion. It tastes rich and special and makes a satisfying morning or afternoon tea treat.

MAKES 1 LOAF   DF

100 g dried apricots, coarsely chopped
100 g dried pitted dates, coarsely chopped
100 g sultanas
50 g raisins
1 cup firmly packed brown sugar
1 cup boiling hot fruit herbal tea infusion

1 small egg, lightly beaten
1 tsp pure vanilla extract
2 cups unbleached spelt flour (or substitute gluten-free baking flour, if preferred)
2 tsp gluten-free baking powder

1. Combine dried fruit and sugar in a bowl. Pour hot tea over and set aside for 30 minutes for the fruits to soften and the liquid to cool.

2. Preheat oven to 180 °C. Line a 1.5-litre capacity loaf tin with non-stick baking paper, leaving an overhang on all sides.

3. Stir beaten egg and vanilla into dried fruit mixture. Sift flour and baking powder into bowl and stir just enough to combine with fruit mixture.

4. Spoon mixture into prepared loaf tin. Bake for 1 hour and 10 minutes, or until loaf tests cooked when a skewer inserted in the centre comes out moist but clean. Cool in the tin for 15 minutes, then remove the loaf to a wire rack to cool completely.

✱ Spelt . . . Spelt flour adds quality nutrients to your baked goods. Spelt is a distant relative to present-day wheat. It is highly water-soluble, so is more easily digested and its nutrients are more readily absorbed by the body. Yes, spelt does contain gluten but it is a more fragile form than wheat gluten, meaning that spelt can be a good alternative for some people with gluten sensitivities but not for people who are allergic to gluten.

Whole Orange Poppy Seed Cakes

Sticky and delicious, these poppy seed cakes are made with the goodness of whole oranges. As a bonus, these treats also happen to be dairy-free and gluten-free and are therefore suitable for those with coeliac disease, people who are gluten-intolerant, or for those who prefer to follow a wheat- or gluten-free diet.

MAKES 12   DF | GF | WF

2 whole oranges
6 small eggs, separated
²/₃ cup raw sugar
⅓ cup liquid honey
3 cups desiccated coconut

¼ cup poppy seeds
1 tsp gluten-free baking powder
1¼ cups Tangy orange syrup
(recipe follows)

1. Coarsely chop oranges, including skin. Remove and discard any seeds and place chopped oranges and any juice in a saucepan with enough cold filtered water to just cover.
2. Bring mixture to the boil then turn down the heat and simmer until the oranges have softened to a pulp and the liquid is almost completely reduced (this will take approximately 40 minutes). Set the mixture aside to cool. Once cold, blend the pulp to form a smooth purée.
3. Preheat oven to 170 °C. Lightly oil 12 x ¾-cup capacity muffin tins or individual cake moulds. Place egg yolks, sugar and honey in a bowl and beat with an electric mixer until thick and creamy. Stir in orange purée, coconut, poppy seeds and baking powder.
4. In a clean bowl, whisk egg whites until soft peaks form. Fold beaten egg whites into cake mixture. Divide mixture between prepared tins and bake for 25 minutes or until a skewer inserted in the centre of one cake comes out clean.
5. Cool cakes in tins for 10 minutes to firm before turning out onto a wire rack to cool completely. Pour hot tangy orange syrup over the cold cakes to coat.

Tangy Orange Syrup

MAKES 1¼ CUPS   DF | EF | GF | WF | V

1 cup orange juice
½ cup lemon juice
stripped zest of 2 oranges
½ cup raw sugar
½ cup honey

1. Place all ingredients in a saucepan. Bring to the boil then simmer for 10–15 minutes or until thick and syrupy.

✳ **Oranges** . . . Oranges are an important source of vitamin C, which is the most important water-soluble antioxidant in the body and is associated with protecting us from disease. The humble orange contains more than 170 phytochemicals, plus they're an excellent source of folate, potassium, soluble and insoluble fibre. Soluble fibre, such as pectin found in oranges, is especially important in lowering the risk of heart disease, diabetes and cancer.

✳ **Zest** . . . Zest is the coloured outer rind (minus the white pith) of citrus fruits, such as lemons, limes, oranges and grapefruit. The zest is particularly potent and can be grated, peeled in strips or shredded off with a gadget called a zester. The zest contains the essential citrus oils and is therefore very fragrant, so use it when you want to add an extra strong citrus zing to desserts and baking.

"How and what we eat can have an astounding effect on how we feel. Food that nourishes us can also provide emotional sustenance."

Happy Family Food

good food for families

✳ **Making meals from scratch** is a great way to eat well, save money and feed the whole family. Another bonus is that you know exactly what has gone into the meals your family is eating. Be creative and continue to build a solid repertoire of foundation recipes, and make changes to core dishes, adding seasonal twists or foods that fussy-eaters particularly enjoy. Be sure to serve variety and colour and cook with foods in their natural state wherever possible. This way, you can minimise the effort needed to get a healthy meal on the table and maximise time spent with your family.

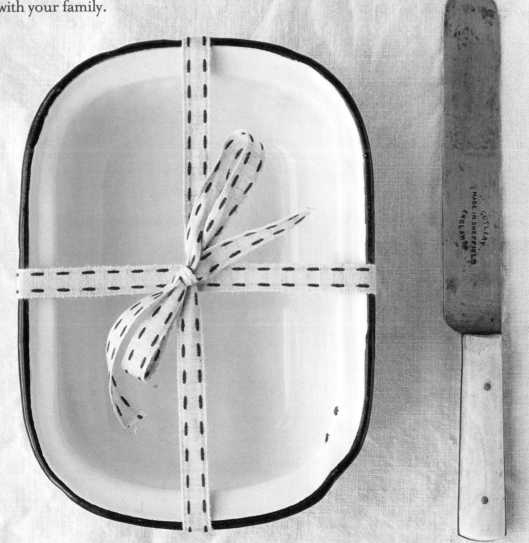

Tomato, Feta and Rocket Pizza

Let the kids into the kitchen so they can experience the pleasure of making something yummy to eat. They will be proud of their achievements and more interested in eating the results. Pizza is a great dish for budding young chefs to start to hone their culinary skills.

SERVES 4 EF | GF | WF

½ recipe Gluten-free pizza dough (recipe follows)
olive oil
gluten-free flour, for dusting
½ cup tomato pasta sauce or tomato purée
5 small tomatoes, thinly sliced
75 g goat's or cow's milk feta, crumbled (or use grated Cheddar, if preferred)

2 tbsp pine nuts
salt and freshly ground black pepper
⅓ cup black olives (optional)
a few fresh rocket leaves or basil leaves, as preferred

1. Preheat oven to 220 °C. Place a baking sheet in the oven to heat – this will help brown the base of the pizza during cooking.

2. Press and shape pizza dough into a large, thin round. Place dough on a lightly oiled cold baking sheet. Using your fingertips, dusted with flour, press dough out thinly and evenly to form a circle or oval shape.

3. Spread base with tomato sauce or purée, leaving the edges free of topping. Top with sliced tomatoes and crumbled feta. Sprinkle over pine nuts and season with salt and pepper. Scatter with olives, if desired, and drizzle with a little oil.

4. Place the baking sheet containing the pizza onto the hot baking sheet in the oven and bake for 25–35 minutes, or until the pizza crust is crisp and golden brown. Remove to a board and scatter with basil or rocket leaves while hot so that the leaves just wilt. Slice and serve immediately.

Gluten-Free Pizza Dough

This dough makes a tasty gluten-free alternative for those who need it and a perfectly good pizza base for those who don't have gluten issues. In fact, it's so thin and crisp they will be unlikely to notice the difference.

MAKES 2 THIN PIZZA BASES   DF | EF | GF | WF | V

1 cup warm filtered water
½ tsp sugar
2 tsp active dry yeast
2½ cups gluten-free flour mix
1 tsp natural sea salt
2 tbsp olive oil
extra gluten-free flour mix, to dust

1. Place warm water in a small bowl. Sprinkle with sugar and yeast and set aside for 5 minutes until the mixture foams, indicating the yeast has been activated.

2. Place flour and salt into the bowl of a food processor. With the motor running, add activated yeast mixture and the oil and process until mixture comes together to form a ball of soft dough. If necessary, add a little more warm water to reach a smooth consistency. (It is unnecessary to knead a gluten-free dough.)

3. Place dough in a lightly oiled bowl. Cover with a damp tea towel and leave in a warm place to rise for approximately one hour, or until doubled in volume.

4. Knock back dough with your fist and turn out onto a work surface lightly dusted with flour and knead just to bring the dough together again. This dough is delicate and hard to roll, so use your hands to press and shape it into the desired-shaped bases and top with your choice of ingredients.

✱ **Kitchen savvy** . . . At this stage, the dough can be stored in the fridge for one day or frozen for up to two weeks. Bring the dough to room temperature before rolling out and cooking.

Light Chicken Meatloaf

Meatloaf is a popular family meal, so here's a lighter version with some clever twists. Made with chicken and bound with high-fibre oats, I've also hidden lots of grated vegetables in here, which is a great way to up the family's vegetable intake without them even realising it. The tomatoes are decorative but when sliced also form a nice juicy sauce for the meatloaf.

SERVES 6   DF | WF

500 g lean chicken mince, preferably organic

1½ cups old-fashioned rolled oats

2 tbsp tomato paste

1 small onion, very finely chopped

1 large carrot, peeled and coarsely grated

1 courgette, trimmed and coarsely grated

2 cloves garlic, crushed

2 tbsp chopped fresh parsley

1 tbsp chopped fresh oregano

2 egg whites

salt and freshly ground black pepper

6 small tomatoes

1. Preheat oven to 180 °C. Line a 1.5-litre-capacity loaf tin with baking paper, leaving an overhang on all sides.

2. Place all ingredients, except tomatoes, in a large bowl and mix with clean hands to combine. Season well with salt and pepper and mix well again.

3. Spoon mixture into prepared tin, pressing down well to compact the mixture. Press tomatoes down halfway into the surface of the mixture.

4. Bake for 60 minutes, or until the juices run clear when a small sharp knife is inserted into the centre of the meatloaf.

5. Cool in the tin for 10 minutes to firm, then use the paper overhang to lift and remove the meatloaf from the tin. Serve hot or refrigerate until cold. Slice to serve.

＊   Natural selection . . . Choose lean chicken for proven health benefits. Breast meat contains less fat than leg meat. And remember, much of the fat is contained in the skin, so it is a healthier choice to go for skinless chicken portions, trimmed of excess fat.

Organic Tomato Sauce

Quick Organic Tomato Sauce

A healthy tomato ketchup is a great accompaniment to many different meals and a good way to disguise some foods or encourage children to try new foods.

MAKES 2 CUPS   DF | EF | GF | WF | V

1 tbsp organic olive oil
2 cloves organic garlic, crushed
400 g chopped organic tomatoes and any juice

¼ cup organic white wine vinegar
⅓ cup organic brown sugar or raw sugar
½ tsp organic sea salt
pinch organic chilli powder

1. Combine all ingredients in a saucepan. Bring just to the boil, stirring regularly until sugar dissolves.
2. Turn down heat and simmer for 10–15 minutes, or until liquid is well reduced. Stir regularly to avoid mixture sticking to pan.
3. Remove to a bowl to cool. This sauce can be served as a chunky mixture or puréed if a smoother sauce is preferred.

* **My advice** . . . Use a very big pot and plenty of water to cook pasta. When the water boils, add a good dose of sea salt for good flavour. There is no need to add oil to the water when cooking pasta, simply stir the pasta into the boiling water to separate the pieces. When the pasta is *al dente* or just tender to the bite, drain it immediately and well to prevent the pasta continuing to absorb water and become gluey.

Spaghetti and Tomato Sauce with Chicken Meatballs

Spaghetti and meatballs has always been an inexpensive, tasty meal the whole family loves. I've packed a few vegetables into this version to keep this fun food healthy and help families up their daily vegetable intake. Plus, these meatballs are made with chicken mince and are baked, so this dish is much lower in saturated fats than the classic version. It can be served as a tasty vegetarian meal, too, if you leave out the meatballs.

SERVES 4   DF

CHICKEN MEATBALLS
500 g lean chicken mince
2 medium carrots, peeled and grated
½ cup fresh wholemeal breadcrumbs
3 cloves garlic, crushed
¼ cup chopped fresh parsley
1 egg white
salt and freshly ground black pepper

TOMATO PASTA SAUCE
2 tbsp olive oil
1 onion, finely diced
2 sticks celery, finely diced

1 medium courgette, trimmed and grated
1 large carrot, trimmed and grated
2 cloves garlic, crushed
600-g can chopped tomatoes (fresh or canned organic)
1 cup liquid vegetable or chicken stock, as perferred
2 tbsp tomato paste
1 tbsp fresh thyme or oregano leaves
salt and freshly ground black pepper

400 g whole-wheat spaghetti pasta

1. To make the meatballs, preheat oven to 190 °C. Line an oven pan with non-stick baking paper. In a bowl, combine ingredients, pounding the mixture with your hands — this helps the meatballs hold together when cooked.

2. With damp hands, shape the mixture into 20 walnut-sized balls. Place meatballs on the prepared oven pan. Bake for 15 minutes, or until golden brown all over and cooked through.

3. To make the sauce, heat oil in a large saucepan, add onion, celery, grated courgette and carrot and cook over medium heat for 10 minutes to soften but not brown. Add garlic and cook for 30 seconds more.

4. Add tomatoes and any juice, stock, tomato paste and thyme or oregano. Bring mixture to the boil then turn down heat and simmer for 10 minutes or until liquid has reduced and mixture is thick. Season with salt and pepper to taste. Stir in the baked chicken meatballs to coat in sauce.

5. At the same time, cook the spaghetti in plenty of boiling, salted water for 8–10 minutes, or according to packet instructions, until just tender to the bite. Drain spaghetti well, and then toss with sauce to coat. Serve immediately.

Layered Pasta Bake

It's a good idea to add some meal ideas like this low-fat, all-in-one dish to your weekly cooking repertoire — then if you're caught short, you'll be able to have this super-tasty and nourishing meal on the table in a relatively short space of time.

SERVES 6 EF

olive oil

¼ cup dry breadcrumbs

1 onion, finely sliced

400-g can organic chopped tomatoes

salt and freshly ground black pepper

300 g spinach, washed with stems removed, coarsely chopped

400 g whole-wheat penne pasta

425-g can tuna in spring water, drained and flaked

2 tbsp chopped fresh oregano

1 cup low-fat cottage cheese

⅓ cup freshly grated Parmesan

Winter pesto, to serve, see page 87 (optional)

1. Preheat oven to 190 °C. Grease a 24-cm springform cake tin with oil. Dust with dry breadcrumbs and shake the tin until surface is evenly coated in crumbs. Shake out and discard any excess crumbs.

2. Heat 2 tablespoons of oil in a pan, add onion and cook for 5 minutes to soften but not brown. Add chopped tomatoes and cook for 5–10 minutes until well reduced and thick. Season with salt and pepper to taste. Wilt the spinach in boiling water for 1 minute then plunge into cold water to cool. Drain and squeeze to remove excess water.

3. At the same time, cook pasta in plenty of boiling, salted water for 7–8 minutes or until just tender to the bite. Drain well and set aside to cool a little.

4. Spoon half the pasta into base of prepared tin and press down firmly. Spread with spinach leaves, scatter with flaked tuna and season between the layers. Spoon the tomato sauce evenly over the top and scatter with the remaining pasta, pressing down firmly.

5. Stir the oregano into the cottage cheese and then spread this over the surface of the top pasta layer. Scatter with Parmesan and bake for 30 minutes or until golden brown. I recommend serving some winter pesto with this dish, if desired.

✳ **My advice** . . . It's easy to ring the changes using a recipe like this one as a base. For example, simply leave out the tuna, if you want to make it a vegetarian dish. Substitute any seasonal vegetables for the spinach, such as chopped broccoli or cauliflower in winter; asparagus in spring; kernels from summer corn; or sliced mushrooms in autumn. Try swapping the Parmesan for feta, Gruyère or Edam, too.

Mediterranean Fisherman's Pie

This popular family-friendly dish with a healthy Mediterranean slant is easy
to make on a weeknight, can appeal to even fussy eaters, and is bound to be
a hit in your household. Use warming everyday recipes like this to survive the
working week, or to share on the weekend with friends and family.

SERVES 6   DF | EF | GF | WF

1.2 kg (6 medium-sized) unpeeled waxy
 potatoes, scrubbed
2 tbsp olive oil, plus extra for brushing the
 potatoes
1 clove garlic, chopped
1 bunch spring onions, finely chopped
2 x 400-g cans chopped tomatoes

¼ cup chopped fresh parsley
2 tbsp chopped fresh basil
¼ cup salted capers, rinsed and drained
 (optional)
salt and freshly ground black pepper
700 g skinless, boneless white fish fillets,
 cut in large pieces

1. Heat oven to 200 °C. Cook the potatoes in boiling, salted water for
10–15 minutes to partially cook. Drain well and set aside. Once cool enough
to handle, thinly slice the potatoes.
2. Heat 2 tablespoons oil in a saucepan. Add the garlic and spring onions
and cook over a medium heat for 2 minutes to soften but not brown. Add
tomatoes and simmer for 5–10 minutes to reduce liquid. Add herbs and
capers, if desired. Season with salt and pepper to taste.
3. Arrange the pieces of fish to cover the base of a deep-sided baking dish.
Spoon over the prepared tomato sauce. Arrange the sliced potatoes in rows to
cover the filling.
4. Drizzle or brush the potatoes with oil. Bake for 30–40 minutes or until
potato topping is golden brown. Serve immediately.

* **Natural selection** . . . There are many health benefits to be gained for the whole
family (including pregnant women) from eating fish regularly. Fresh fish is believed to
be a brain food and so aim for two or more servings of fish a week for good health.

Chicken Pie with Scone–Style Pastry Crust

Big on taste and texture, this healthy dish offers a highly nourishing and satisfying meal solution to keep your family happy, healthy and well fed. Playing with the cut of vegetables makes food more interesting for children, too. Try chopping each vegetable into a different shape, as this will make the food fun.

SERVES 4   DF

olive oil
1 leek, sliced
2 carrots, sliced
2 stalks celery, sliced
600 g skinless chicken breasts,
   cut in 2-cm cubes
2 cups liquid chicken stock
2 tbsp cornflour

⅓ cup cold filtered water
1 cup peas (fresh or frozen)
2 tbsp chopped fresh parsley
salt and freshly ground black
   pepper
Scone–style pastry (recipe
   follows)

1. Preheat oven to 200 °C. Heat a saucepan, add a little oil, leek, carrots and celery and cook over medium heat for 5 minutes, stirring frequently. Remove to one side. Add a little more oil and brown the chicken in two batches. Remove chicken to one side.
2. Pour chicken stock into the pan, stirring to remove any flavoursome sediment from the bottom. Mix the cornflour with the cold water to form a smooth paste. Add to the pan and simmer for 5 minutes, stirring continuously until sauce thickens.
3. Return chicken and vegetables to pan. Stir in peas and parsley and season with salt and pepper to taste. Spoon hot chicken mixture into a 1.5-litre pie dish.
4. Roll out pastry 5-mm thick until it is just larger than the top of the pie dish to form a lid for the pie. Trim and crimp edges with a fork to secure the pastry lid. Cut a few small slits in the surface of the pastry to allow steam to escape during cooking.
5. Bake for 30 minutes or until pastry is golden brown. Remove from oven and serve piping hot.

* My advice . . . Make sure any chicken pie leftovers are heated through until they are piping hot and don't reheat any food more than once.

Scone-Style Pastry

This pastry works well with either ordinary flour or gluten-free flour, but will naturally have a different texture depending on the type of flour you choose.

MAKES ENOUGH FOR 1 PIE CRUST   DF

2 cups spelt flour, or plain all-purpose flour,
   or gluten-free flour, as preferred
2 tsp gluten-free baking powder
½ tsp salt
2 tbsp olive oil
½ cup cold filtered water
1 large egg, lightly beaten

1. Sift flour, baking powder and salt into a bowl. Add oil, water and beaten egg and mix well. The mixture will be crumbly, but moist. Knead very briefly, just enough to bring mixture together and form into a flat disc.

Jacket Potatoes Filled with Home-Baked Beans

This recipe shows that healthy food doesn't have to be boring or expensive. Baked potatoes in their jackets are a good source of energy — and stuffed baked potatoes are particularly delicious. Half the fun is in the making, so if you can guide your children into learning to cook, and get them to sit down with you for regular family meals, then you will set them up with healthy eating patterns for life.

SERVES 4   EF | GF | WF

4 very large baking potatoes, scrubbed

olive oil

salt and freshly ground black pepper

Home-baked beans (recipe follows)

100 g crumbled feta or ½ cup grated Cheddar

¼ cup fresh parsley leaves

1. Preheat oven to 200 °C. Choose potatoes that are the same size, so they cook evenly. For a crispy skin, rub potatoes lightly all over with a little oil and season with salt and pepper.

2. Pierce each potato with the tip of a sharp knife several times — this allows moisture to escape and stops the potatoes exploding during baking.

3. Place potatoes in an oven pan and bake for 1 hour or until tender. Remove potatoes from oven, slice in half and carefully scoop out flesh. Mash potato flesh and season with salt and pepper.

4. Place mashed potato into potato skins. Top with a big spoonful of baked beans. Scatter with cheese of choice and bake for 15 minutes more or until potatoes are piping hot and cheese is golden brown. Serve scattered with parsley.

Home-Baked Beans

Homemade baked beans can be served as a meal in themselves for supper, or try them as a breakfast, brunch or lunch dish.

SERVES 4   DF | EF | GF | WF | V

2 tbsp olive oil

1 large onion, finely diced

3 cloves garlic, chopped

1 tbsp brown sugar

2 tbsp red wine vinegar

2 bay leaves

2 x 400-g cans chopped tomatoes

420-g can white cannellini beans rinsed, and drained

1 tbsp chopped fresh thyme

salt and freshly ground black pepper

1. Preheat oven to 200 °C. Place all ingredients, except salt and pepper, into an ovenproof dish.

2. Cover dish and bake for 45 minutes (bake alongside jacket potatoes).

3. Remove from oven, taste and adjust seasoning with salt and pepper.

4. Serve baked beans as a meal in themselves, or spoon over baked potatoes.

Family Frittata

Frittata is an Italian form of omelette and is a great dish to have as a base recipe. You can change out the vegetables for any that are in season or for those the kids will eat. For example, use sliced tomato or courgette instead of asparagus. You can even add peas, corn or carrots to this frittata if these are vegetables the children like.

SERVES 6 GF | WF

450 g (2 medium-sized) kumara, peeled and cut into chunks

185-g can tuna in spring water, drained and flaked

4 spring onions, chopped

5 large eggs

½ cup milk of your choice (low-fat milk is fine, too)

¼ cup chopped fresh parsley

salt and freshly ground black pepper

150 g asparagus, trimmed and cut in half

75 g cow's or goat's milk feta, crumbled (or use grated Cheddar, if preferred)

1. Preheat oven to 190 °C. Line a 22-cm round cake tin with baking paper, leaving an overhang on all sides. Cook kumara in boiling, salted water for 5 minutes until just tender. Drain and set aside to cool a little.

2. Scatter kumara over base of prepared tin. Scatter over tuna and spring onions.

3. In a bowl, lightly beat eggs, then add milk and parsley. Season well with salt and pepper and whisk to combine.

4. Pour egg mixture over vegetables and tuna. Arrange sliced asparagus over surface and scatter with crumbled feta or grated Cheddar.

5. Bake for 35–40 minutes or until set and pale golden brown. Cut into wedges and serve warm or cold.

* My advice . . . Any leftover roast vegetables, such as potatoes, pumpkin, carrots or a mixture, work well in place of the kumara, if desired.

Fish Ball Soup

SERVES 4   DF | EF | GF | WF

400 g boneless white-fleshed fish, roughly cubed
¼ cup ground almonds
2 cloves garlic, crushed
1 small red chilli, seeds removed, finely chopped (optional)
3-cm piece ginger, finely grated
4 spring onions, finely chopped
¼ cup chopped fresh parsley
salt and freshly ground black pepper
1 litre liquid fish or chicken stock
juice of 1 lemon

1. Place cubed fish in the bowl of a food processor and
process to form a rough textured paste.
2. Transfer to a bowl and combine with remaining ingredients,
except the stock and lemon juice. Season with salt and
pepper and mix well.
3. With damp hands, shape mixture into 24 walnut-sized balls.
Place stock in a large saucepan and bring to the boil. Add
fish balls and turn down heat.
4. Simmer gently for 8 minutes to cook fish balls. Add lemon
juice to soup and adjust seasoning with salt and pepper, if
necessary. Serve immediately.

Chicken Noodle Soup

SERVES 4   DF

1.5 litres liquid chicken stock
200 g lean chicken mince
100 g soba noodles
salt and freshly ground black pepper
¼ cup chopped fresh herbs, such as basil, chives, parsley or
    coriander

1. Place stock in saucepan and bring to the boil. Add chicken
mince and noodles and stir to separate.
2. Turn down heat and simmer for 5 minutes or until noodles
are just tender to the bite.
3. Taste soup and, if needed, adjust seasoning with salt and
pepper. Serve in big bowls sprinkled with chopped fresh herbs

Chinese Corn and Egg Soup

SERVES 4   DF | GF | WF

1 litre liquid chicken stock
2 cups sweet corn kernels
3 tbsp cornflour
⅓ cup cold filtered water
2 egg whites, lightly beaten
1 tsp cold-pressed sesame oil
salt and freshly ground black pepper
4 spring onions, finely sliced

1. Place stock in a saucepan and bring to the boil. Add corn kernels and simmer for 5 minutes.
2. Mix cornflour with cold water to form a smooth paste. Add this paste to the soup and stir continuously for 3 minutes until soup thickens.
3. Add beaten egg whites to hot soup in a thin stream, stirring continuously. Season with oil and salt and pepper to taste. Serve topped with sliced spring onions.

Alphabet Soup

SERVES 6   DF | V

2 tbsp olive oil
3 cloves garlic, crushed
1 litre tomato juice, preferably organic
2 cups liquid vegetable stock or vegetable cooking water
½ cup alphabet pasta or other tiny pasta shapes
salt and freshly ground black pepper

1. Heat oil in a saucepan. Add garlic and cook over medium heat for 30 seconds.
2. Add tomato juice and vegetable stock to pan and bring to the boil. Add pasta and simmer for 10 minutes until pasta is *al dente*.
3. Season with salt and pepper to taste. Serve piping hot in big bowls.

✳ **The best soup** . . . Use good-quality ingredients to produce the best soups. For maximum flavour, use homemade, organic or good-quality store-bought liquid stock.

set of 4
pudding
bowls

Pure Puddings

guilt-free delights

✻ **Sweet and saucy**, hot and gooey, puddings are heart-warming treats. These puddings are made with natural ingredients and lots of fresh fruit, so occasionally ending a meal with something sweet doesn't have to be a guilty indulgence. A good dessert, whether simple or spectacular, will always end a meal with a flourish. The sticky deliciousness or fresh fruit fabulousness of the results, and the fact that you've made it yourself with love, will naturally impress friends and family.

Meringue-Topped Fruit Puddings

This crisp meringue topping has just enough crunch to complement the syrupy fruit mixture that lies beneath. While this is a great fruit combination, any other stewed fruits can be substituted for the apples and berries, if desired. Try plums, apricots, nectarines or peaches, rhubarb, pears or any combination of seasonal fruits at hand.

SERVES 6   DF | GF | WF

2 apples, peeled and cored
⅓ cup honey
¼ cup cold filtered water
2 cups blackberries, raspberries or
   blueberries

MERINGUE
3 egg whites
1 tsp pure vanilla extract
1 cup caster sugar

1. Preheat oven to 200 °C. Cut apples into cubes and place in a saucepan with honey and water. Cover pan and cook over a low heat for 5 minutes.

2. Remove pan from heat and stir in berries. Divide fruit mixture between six ramekins, tea or coffee cups or heatproof glasses.

3. To make meringue, place egg whites in a clean bowl and whisk with an electric beater until soft peaks form. Add vanilla extract, then gradually add sugar while continuing to whisk for 2 minutes or until mixture is thick and glossy.

4. Spoon some meringue on top of each ramekin of fruit, making sure it reaches the edges of the dish. Bake for 5–8 minutes or until tips of meringue are golden brown. Serve hot or warm.

✳ My advice . . . Use good-quality honey to sweeten stewed fruits instead of sugar. Honey is not only a natural sweetener that energises the body, it is also a powerful antioxidant that can help boost immunity and promote healing.

Cherry Clafoutis

Warming and homely, there's nothing as pleasing as a spongy, fruity, custard pudding! This one is a French classic studded with fresh cherries, though you can use any seasonal fruit. My version is lighter and healthier than the original recipe. Plus, because this fruity pudding has a light custard base, it needs no other accompaniment.

SERVES 6

I tsp light olive oil, to grease dish
2 small eggs, at room temperature
¼ cup caster sugar
I tsp pure vanilla extract
pinch of salt

⅓ cup milk
¼ cup spelt or wheat flour
18 fresh cherries (whole or pitted, as preferred)
icing sugar, to dust

I. Preheat oven to 180 °C. Brush base and sides of a 20-cm flan dish lightly with oil. Place eggs, sugar, vanilla and salt in a bowl and beat with an electric mixer until thick and pale.

2. On a low speed, beat in milk and then flour, to just combine. Pour mixture into prepared dish and scatter cherries over the top.

3. Bake for 20 minutes or until puffed and golden brown. Remove from oven and dust with icing sugar. Serve hot.

✱ Natural selection . . . Delectable sweet and sour cherries are high in fibre, which helps promote digestive health. Cherries contain no cholesterol and can even assist in regulating blood pressure. Also containing potassium, iron, riboflavin and vitamin C, the cherries pack a good nutritional punch.

Rhubarb and Blueberry Crisp

Similar to a crumble, a fruit crisp is very easy to make and very comforting to eat. This rhubarb and berry version, with its crisp, crunchy topping, lives up to both these expectations. Plus, unlike most crumbles, this dish is relatively low in sugar and fat, so it makes a great choice for a family pudding.

SERVES 6 DF | EF | WF | V

¼ cup cold filtered water
¾ cup raw sugar
700 g trimmed rhubarb, cut in 2-cm lengths
2 cups blueberries (fresh or frozen)
1 tbsp light olive oil

1 tsp pure vanilla extract
2 tbsp honey
2 tbsp soft brown sugar
1 cup old-fashioned rolled oats
icing sugar, to dust

1. Preheat oven to 180 °C. Place water and raw sugar in a saucepan and bring to the boil, stirring until sugar dissolves. Add rhubarb and blueberries and simmer for 5 minutes to poach.

2. Remove fruit to a 1.5-litre capacity ceramic, ovenproof dish, or divide between 6 individual ramekins or ovenproof bowls — coffee cups are also ovenproof and make a fun way to serve these as individual puddings.

3. Heat oil, vanilla, honey and brown sugar in a saucepan until dissolved and combined, stirring continuously. Stir in the oats, to coat. Sprinkle mixture over the fruit base.

4. Bake for 25–30 minutes, or until fruit is bubbling hot and the topping is crisp and lightly browned. Dust with icing sugar, if desired, and serve immediately.

✳ Kitchen savvy . . . Frozen berries make a great standby to have on hand over the winter months. A few berries will add colour, flavour and goodness to many dishes, like this simple fruit crisp.

Lemony Fruit Pudding

This amazing pudding has a lovely fruity base covered with a sweet-sour lemon topping that magically separates into layers of lemon custard, spongy textured pudding and a meringue-like crust. By only adding a little sugar to the fruit it stays quite tart, which is a nice foil for the sweet lemony pudding that envelops it.

SERVES 6 DF

12 small plums, halved with stones removed
½ cup Craisins
1 cup cold filtered water
⅓ cup raw sugar

LEMON TOPPING

2 large eggs
½ cup caster sugar
juice and finely grated zest of 2 lemons
¼ cup spelt flour (or substitute plain flour, if preferred)
icing sugar, to dust

1. Combine plums, Craisins, water and sugar in a saucepan and simmer gently for about 20 minutes or until fruit is soft and pulpy and water is greatly reduced (the fruit will be almost jam-like). Watch carefully, and stir regularly while cooking so that the mixture does not boil dry or stick to the pan. Set aside to cool.

2. Preheat oven to 160 °C. Transfer cooled fruit mixture to the base of a 1.5-litre capacity ovenproof pie dish.

3. To make lemon topping, beat eggs and sugar together in a bowl with an electric mixer until thick and pale. Gently beat in lemon juice and zest and then beat in flour.

4. Pour mixture over prepared fruit. Bake for 45 minutes or until lemon topping is set. Dust with a little icing sugar and serve hot or warm.

✽ My advice . . . Any seasonal fruit can be used in place of the plums in this fruity pudding. Try peaches or apricots or any berry fruits in the summertime. Over the winter months use rhubarb, apples, pears or even frozen berries for their vibrant colour and goodness.

Very Berry Coconut Tartlets

SERVES 6   GF | WF

115 g butter, softened
½ cup caster sugar
2 small eggs
1½ cups fine desiccated coconut
2 tbsp tapioca flour or gluten-free baking flour
2 cups mixed fresh berries, such as blueberries, blackberries,
    strawberries and raspberries
gluten-free icing sugar, to dust

1. Preheat oven to 180 °C. Line six 10-cm tartlet tins with non-stick baking paper. In a bowl, beat butter and sugar together until pale and creamy.
2. Add eggs one at a time, beating well after each addition. Stir in coconut and flour to just combine. Spread mixture over base of tartlet tins, dividing it evenly. Sprinkle surface of each with berries.
3. Bake for 30–35 minutes, or until set in the middle and golden brown. Serve hot or cold, dusted with icing sugar.

Strawberry Yoghurt Parfaits

SERVES 4   EF | GF | WF

3 cups fresh strawberries
3 tbsp caster sugar
1 cup Toasted almond granola (see recipe page 21)
¼ cup brandy, or liqueur of your choice
2 cups plain unsweetened Greek-style yoghurt

1. Hull strawberries, leaving 8 intact for decoration. Purée 1 cup of strawberries with the sugar. Finely chop remaining strawberries.
2. Alternate layers of granola sprinkled with a little brandy or liqueur, strawberry purée, chopped strawberries and yoghurt in 4 glasses.
3. Chill for 30 minutes (or longer, if desired) before serving. Top each parfait with two reserved strawberries to decorate.

✳ My advice . . . Frozen at their peak to capture all their nutrients and goodness, frozen berries are just as good as fresh. Add fresh or frozen berries to puddings and enjoy the benefits of their high antioxidant powers.

Berry Chiffon Pudding Cakes

MAKES 6

2 egg whites
⅓ cup caster sugar
1 tsp pure vanilla extract
2 tbsp light olive oil
½ cup low-fat plain unsweetened yoghurt
1½ cups mixed berries (fresh or frozen)
1 cup plain flour
¾ tsp baking soda
icing sugar, to dust

1. Preheat oven to 180 °C. Lightly spray six ¾-cup capacity cake or muffin tins with olive oil.
2. In a clean bowl, beat egg whites until soft peaks hold their shape. Fold in sugar and vanilla and then the oil, yoghurt and half the berries. Sift flour and baking soda into bowl and stir just enough to combine.
3. Spoon mixture into prepared tins and scatter with remaining berries. Bake for 25–30 minutes, or until firm and golden brown.
4. Serve warm, dusted with icing sugar and with extra yoghurt on the side, if desired.

Vanilla Berry Yoghurt Brûlée

SERVES 4   EF | GF | WF

3 cups mixed berries, such as blueberries, blackberries, strawberries and raspberries
2 tbsp brandy, or liqueur of your choice (optional)
1 tsp pure vanilla extract
1 cup plain unsweetened yoghurt
½ cup caster sugar

1. Divide berries between four shallow, ovenproof dishes. Sprinkle each with a little brandy or liqueur, if desired. Preheat a grill to high (or use a culinary blowtorch, if you have one).
2. Mix vanilla into yoghurt. Spread a quarter of a cup of yoghurt over berries in each dish. Sprinkle sugar liberally over yoghurt. Place dishes on an oven sheet.
3. Place under grill for 4–5 minutes, or until sugar has caramelised and turned golden brown.

Rosy Cranberry Poached Pears

When pears are poached in cranberry juice, they take on a delicate pink colouring and heightened taste that takes them from simple to special in a couple of easy steps. Perfumed and pretty, poached pears make a very elegant dessert.

SERVES 6   DF | EF | GF | WF | V

1 litre cranberry or pomegranate juice, as preferred

1 litre filtered cold water

1 cup raw sugar or honey, as perferred

peeled rind and juice of 1 lemon

6 large firm pears, peeled to retain stalks

1 tbsp rosewater

a few dried rosebuds, to decorate (optional)

1. Combine cranberry or pomegranate juice, water, sugar or honey, lemon rind and juice in a saucepan and bring to the boil. Add pears and then turn down heat and reduce to a simmer. Place a piece of baking paper on top of pears to make sure they are fully submerged in liquid.

2. Poach in this way for 25 minutes or until pears are just tender. Remove pears to a serving dish to cool.

3. Strain cooking liquid to remove and discard flavourings. Return liquid to pan, bring to the boil and then turn down heat to simmer hard for 10–20 minutes or until the liquid is reduced to a thick syrup.

4. Lastly, stir in the rosewater and pour the syrup over pears. Set aside to cool. Decorate with a few dried rosebuds, if desired. Serve warm or cold.

* Cranberries . . . These crimson-coloured super berries have a refreshing sweet-tart flavour and lots of proven health benefits. They are full of polyphenols, which are potent antioxidants that help protect our bodies against heart disease and other diseases. Clinical research shows that drinking cranberry juice every day can help to prevent urinary tract infections and inflammation, due to a unique enzyme specific to cranberries.

Fine Apple Tart

This classic French tart, with its neat rows of thinly sliced apples cooked until golden brown, is a great favourite of mine. For that professional finishing touch and for added flavour, I like to glaze the apples with hot apricot jam.

SERVES 6   EF

1 pre-rolled puff pastry sheet, thawed from
   frozen
4 Royal Gala apples, peeled and cored
20 g butter, melted

2 tbsp caster sugar
¼ cup apricot jam
juice of 1 lemon

1. Heat oven to 200 °C. Place puff pastry sheet on a baking tray. Using a large plate as a guide, cut pastry into a large round. Discard the trimmings. Prick the pastry circle all over with a fork to stop it puffing up when cooked.
2. Thinly slice apples. Arrange slices in circles on top of the pastry, overlapping slightly, until pastry is covered. Brush surface of apple with melted butter and evenly sprinkle with a light dusting of sugar.
3. Bake for 30 minutes or until pastry and apples are cooked and golden brown. Remove tart from oven. Glaze and serve hot or warm.
4. To make apricot glaze, place apricot jam and lemon juice in a small saucepan. Stir over heat until jam melts. Sieve mixture to produce a smooth glaze. Brush glaze evenly over apples while glaze is still hot.

✳   **Good idea** . . . As a rule of thumb, apples with higher natural sweetness, such as Golden Delicious or Royal Gala, will hold their shape when cooked as sugar strengthens the apple's shape-holding properties. If you want a collapsed purée of apples, use a less sweet variety, such as Granny Smith.

Chocolate Prune Puddings

Containing no butter or oil, just two eggs and some quality chocolate, these puddings retain all the gooey chocolate appeal of any chocolate treat but with a lot less fat per serve. The prune mixture gives the puddings a lovely chewy texture and replaces any need for butter. Distinctive individual puddings like these seem to be particularly appealing and there's no more work involved in spooning the mix into individual cooking vessels beforehand, than there is to divide the finished product.

SERVES 6

100 g (½ cup) chopped pitted prunes
1 cup cold filtered water
100 g good-quality dark eating chocolate, coarsely chopped
¼ cup black coffee
2 large eggs
½ cup firmly packed soft brown sugar
1 tsp pure vanilla extract
½ cup wholemeal flour
1 tsp baking soda
¼ cup cocoa powder, sifted
Chocolate maple sauce (recipe follows), to serve

1. Preheat oven to 180 °C. Set six 1-cup capacity ramekins on an oven tray. Place prunes and water in a small saucepan over medium–low heat and simmer until prunes are very tender and liquid has mostly reduced. Remove mixture to a bowl to cool.
2. Place chocolate and coffee in a heatproof bowl set over a saucepan of gently simmering water to melt. Or microwave in short bursts until melted. Stir until smooth then combine with the prune mixture.
3. Place eggs, sugar and vanilla in a bowl and whisk with an electric mixer until thick and pale. Fold in the chocolate prune mixture. Add flour, baking soda and cocoa and gently fold into chocolate mixture just enough to combine.
4. Spoon mixture into prepared dishes. Bake for 20 minutes or until a skewer inserted in the centre of one comes out moist but clean. Drizzle with chocolate maple sauce and enjoy!

Chocolate Maple Sauce

I came up with this idea of using healthy maple syrup in place of the cream usually used to make a chocolate ganache. The maple syrup adds a nice touch of sweetness to the bitter chocolate and, amazingly, this beautiful glossy sauce stays nice and gooey without setting.

MAKES ⅔ CUP   DF | EF | GF | WF | V

100 g quality dark eating chocolate (dairy-free), coarsely chopped
¼ cup maple syrup

1. Place chocolate and maple syrup in a heatproof bowl set over a saucepan of gently simmering water to melt. Alternatively, microwave in short bursts until melted.
2. Stir until smooth and serve hot, drizzled over warm puddings.

✳ **Kitchen savvy** . . . Chocolate will melt more easily if it is chopped into small even-sized pieces beforehand. Use a large, heavy knife to chop the chocolate on a clean, dry board.

✳ **Wholemeal flour** . . . Wholemeal flour is high in fibre, which is important for digestive health plus it makes you feel full longer. Wholemeal flour also has a low glycemic index (GI), which means it gives a sustained energy release keeping blood-sugar levels even.

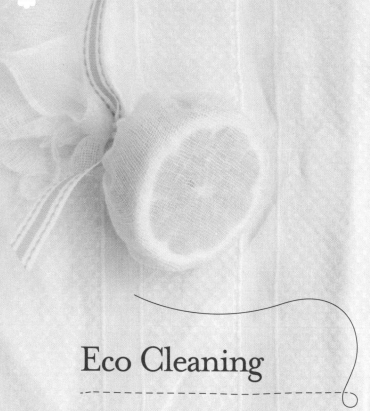

Eco Cleaning

Using natural ingredients is an excellent way to keep kitchens germ-free without chemicals. I've rediscovered that it's possible to thoroughly clean my house naturally with products that are not only safe and gentle for humans, but also kind to the planet.

There's nothing new to this idea. These are actually old-fashioned tried and true cleaning methods that are exactly what our grandmothers once did. Changing to eco cleaning needn't be an inconvenience. In fact, it can feel wonderful to de-clutter and get back to basics. Cutting down on unnecessary chemicals is better for you, your family and the environment.

The two key products you need to keep your house spic and span without hurting the planet or your family are nothing more than baking soda and distilled white vinegar. You'll probably already have these low-cost items in your kitchen pantry, making it even easier to make a few adjustments to your cleaning routine in order to live a cleaner, greener life.

Baking Soda

Also known as bicarbonate of soda or sodium bicarbonate, baking soda is a natural, inexpensive, common baking ingredient and an effective, non-toxic solution to everyday cleaning. This is the first item you need to keep your kitchen clean, germ-free and odour-free — without resorting to chemicals. Here are some of the many valuable ways baking soda can work.

Use dry baking soda as a deep-cleaning but gentle abrasive powder. For hard to shift dirt, baking soda becomes even more powerful if mixed with some lemon juice or distilled white vinegar. To remove unpleasant odours, sprinkle baking soda over carpets, leave for an

hour and then vacuum clean. You can deodorise rubbish bins with a sprinkling of baking soda, too. A solution of baking soda and warm water can be used to clean tea and coffee stains from china cups and to remove burnt-on food from pans. A paste of baking soda and water can be used to polish chrome, and clean the oven, and will also remove mould from surfaces and fabrics.

Distilled White Vinegar

White vinegar kills bacteria, which is where odours come from. Dilute vinegar with an equal quantity of water and use as a cleansing surface spray to cut through grease, disinfect, deodorise and remove mould and mildew. This spray is also excellent for cleaning and deodorising the fridge and microwave oven.

Add a drop of liquid detergent to diluted vinegar to make a window-cleaning spray and rub off with crumpled newspaper for a sparkling finish. Pour neat vinegar down drains to deodorise them; leave for 30 minutes then flush through with cold water. Blot fresh stains, such as red wine, immediately and then sponge with undiluted vinegar to remove the stain.

A Few Other Useful Natural Cleaning Items

* Lemon juice mixed with baking soda will remove stains and clean brass. Lemon juice is also a natural bleaching agent.

* Eco-friendly liquid soap for washing hands, boards and dishes.

* Refillable spray bottles are very useful to mix dilutions and disperse natural cleaning solutions.

* Rags can be used as bench wipes, dusters and polishing cloths. To properly sanitise cleaning cloths, be sure to wash them regularly in boiling water.

* Natural beeswax polish for wooden furniture, especially to care for antiques.

Basic Food Safety

These concepts may be common sense to some, but it's always good to be reminded of the basics, especially when it relates to the health and safety of those we love.

Cleanliness is essential. Top of the list is to wash your hands, often. Use hot, soapy water and dry your hands well, especially before and after food preparation. Use a separate towel for drying your hands and change and wash dishcloths and tea towels every day. Keep them germ-free by boiling them in water with a teaspoonful of distilled white vinegar and baking soda.

To prevent cross contamination, wash your hands, preparation surfaces, and anything that comes in contact with raw meat and poultry (knives, chopping boards, etc.) in hot, soapy water and dry between uses.

I use wooden chopping boards, as these contain natural antibacterial qualities but it is important to always scrub chopping boards well with hot soapy water after each use. It is also wise to keep boards used for vegetables separate from those used for raw meats, fish and poultry. I like to reserve a different board for fruit, so that it doesn't take on any savoury flavours, such as the taste of onions.

Keep food, especially protein-rich foods (meat, poultry, eggs) out of the danger zone; that is, at warm temperatures when bacteria is likely to grow. Cool food promptly to room temperature and then refrigerate. Defrost frozen food, especially poultry, in the fridge and not on the kitchen bench. Cover and store raw and cooked foods separately in the fridge to prevent any raw food juices dripping onto cooked food and contaminating it.

Cover foods to keep out dirt and insects. Avoid plastic if you can and choose reusable food covers, like plates to cover bowls and glass or wire cake covers.

When in doubt, throw it out – don't take the risk of serving any food you may be unsure of.

How to Read a Food Label

The information on food labels can help you make wise food choices. When buying packaged food, check the label information carefully. Once you start doing this it becomes a constant curiosity to see what's in the food you're buying. First off, you might not know what to look for, so here's a short list of the most important information to scrutinise.

Look at the ingredients list panel. The ingredients are listed in order of proportions, so the first item listed is the main ingredient in the product, and so on. If sugar, fat or salt are high on the list then this indicates that the product may not be all that healthy. Avoid products that are high in chemical preservatives and harmful trans fats. Look for ingredients that you or your family may be allergic to so you can avoid these, of course. A short ingredient list may mean the food is less processed and will probably be a healthier choice.

Next, check the nutritional makeup of the food in the fact panel, shown in percentages. Look for foods that have a high percentage of fibre, vitamins and minerals and are low in saturated fats, sodium (salt) and sugar. The pack will also give a suggested serving size and it's wise to make sure this is close to the amount you usually serve and eat.

Food labels will also tell you other useful facts, such as whether the product is certified organic; where the product is made; and what country the ingredients are from, so you can choose to buy local products made in your own country.

"The two key products you need to keep your house spic and span without hurting the planet or your family are nothing more than baking soda and distilled white vinegar."

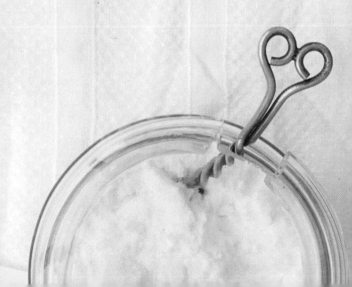

PENGUIN BOOKS
Published by the Penguin Group
Penguin Group (NZ), 67 Apollo Drive, Rosedale,
    North Shore 0632, New Zealand (a division of
    Pearson New Zealand Ltd)
Penguin Group (USA) Inc., 375 Hudson Street,
    New York, New York 10014, USA
Penguin Group (Canada), 90 Eglinton Avenue East,
    Suite 700, Toronto, Ontario, M4P 2Y3, Canada (a division
    of Pearson Penguin Canada Inc.)
Penguin Books Ltd, 80 Strand, London, WC2R 0RL, England
Penguin Ireland, 25 St Stephen's Green,
    Dublin 2, Ireland (a division of Penguin Books Ltd)
Penguin Group (Australia), 250 Camberwell Road,
    Camberwell,
Victoria 3124, Australia (a division of Pearson Australia
    Group Pty Ltd)
Penguin Books India Pvt Ltd, 11, Community Centre,
    Panchsheel Park, New Delhi – 110 017, India
Penguin Books (South Africa) (Pty) Ltd, 24 Sturdee Avenue,
    Rosebank, Johannesburg 2196, South Africa

Penguin Books Ltd, Registered Offices: 80 Strand, London,
    WC2R 0RL, England

First published by Penguin Group (NZ), 2010
1 3 5 7 9 10 8 6 4 2

Text and photography © Julie Le Clerc, 2010

The right of Julie Le Clerc to be identified as the author of
this work in terms of section 96 of the Copyright Act 1994 is
hereby asserted.

Designed by Seven
Prepress by Image Centre Ltd
Printed in China through Bookbuilders, Hong Kong
Printed on paper from sustainable forests

ISBN: 9 78 0 14320464 0

A catalogue record for this book is available
from the National Library of New Zealand.

www.penguin.co.nz

www.julieleclerc.com

Acknowledgements

I wish to extend my heartfelt thanks to those who have supported me during the creation and production of this book. I consider myself very fortunate to work with people I hugely respect and admire.

My warmest thanks go to Bernice Beachman, consulting publisher to Penguin Books, for your extraordinary sense of style and brilliant ideas. The notion of this clever cover is another one of your triumphs! And thanks for cups of tea and conversation on location, along with supplying endlessly fabulous props.

Thank you to the talented team at Penguin Books NZ, publisher Jeff Atkinson and editor Emma Beckett, for your loyal support and the invaluable help you send my way. Thank you kindly to editor, Louise Russell, for your encouragement of my work and for your excellent editing skills. To the design team at Seven, thanks for bringing everything together and creating this book's original arrangement and user-friendly feel.

Thank you to my friends and family for understanding my need to focus on this project and for being there at the end to celebrate. Thank you sweet Sophia Newth for lending your lovely hands to grace the pages of this book — you're a real star! Grateful thanks to Meredith Lee of European Antiques, for the loan of extra special props from your private collection. And thank you to all the numerous and willing eaters who form my trusted tasting panel and provide feedback during the recipe-testing process. You know who you are!

I'd also like to say a big thank you to Ocean Spray for showing me first-hand the wonders of the cranberry, an extraordinary super fruit, and for producing super cranberry products.

Deepest thanks go to my parents, Brian and Loraine Le Clerc, for your constant love and support and for sowing early seeds of inspiration that have grown over my lifetime. Thank you, Dad, for teaching me about gardening; for taking me fishing; and for showing me the value of these simple, sustaining pleasures. Thank you, Mum, not only for teaching me to cook with flavour, but for letting me loose in the kitchen from a young age; and for sharing your special gift of made-by-hand creativity. This book is for you both, with my love and gratitude.

✱ **Julie Le Clerc** is well-known for creating innovative flavours and trusted recipes you can rely on. As a former café owner, caterer and chef, Julie was able to develop and express her own individual recipe style before turning her talents to food writing. Now this award-winning author's life is dedicated to the pursuit of good food and culinary travel. Reflecting her background and influences, Julie's cookbooks are filled with accessible, uncomplicated, clever recipes that encourage keen home cooks to put together nourishing and flavoursome dishes from scratch.

And as the food editor for Next magazine, Julie delivers even more of her inspiring recipes to readers each month.

Also an accomplished photographer, Julie enjoys capturing her own food and styling on film — as well as eclectic collections of her favourite ingredients and kitchen things. Her charming images decorate the pages of this book.

www.julieleclerc.com